COMMUNITY, EUCHARIST, AND SPIRITUALITY

Kenan B. Osborne, OFM

D1403516

Liguori

Liguori, Missouri

Imprimi Potest: Thomas D. Picton, C.Ss.R.
Provincial, Denver Province • The Redemptorists

Published by Liguori • Liguori, Missouri • www.liguori.org

Library of Congress Cataloging-in-Publication Data

Osborne, Kenan B.
  Community, Eucharist, and spirituality / Kenan B. Osborne. — 1st ed.
    p. cm.
  Included index.
  ISBN 978-0-7648-1557-7
  1. Lord's Supper—Catholic Church. 2. Spirituality—Catholic Church.
  3. Communities—Religious aspects—Christianity. I. Title.
  BX2215.3.O83 2007
  234´.163—dc22   2006039562

Liguori Publications, a nonprofit corporation, is an apostolate of the Redemptorists. To learn more about the Redemptorists, visit *Redemptorists.com.*

Printed in the United States of America
11 10 09 08 07   5 4 3 2 1
First edition

Contents

Contents

Introduction

On Saturday, June 4, 2005, a lecture series entitled *Spirituality for the 21st Century* took place in Kansas City, Missouri, under the auspices of the Catholic Community Foundation. In 2006, these lectures were published by Liguori Publications in a volume entitled *Spirituality for the 21st Century: Experiencing God in the Catholic Tradition.* The editor of this volume was Richard W. Miller II. The authors of these lectures included a number of distinguished theologians: Rev. Michael J. Buckley, S.J., Dr. Colleen Griffith, Rev. Michael J. Himes, Dr. Mary Ann Hinsdale, and Msgr. John J. Strynkowski. I was privileged to be included as a lecturer with these notable men and women.

Shortly after the lectures, Daniel Michaels, acquisitions editor at Liguori Publications, contacted me and asked whether I would be willing to elaborate on the theme of my own contribution, "Spirituality and Eucharist," and to develop it into a book. I agreed, and this volume is the result of my efforts.

The major theme of this volume can be stated in a few words: without a viable and gospel Christian community, neither the celebration of Mass nor a eucharistic spirituality has any meaning whatsoever. These three issues—community, Eucharist, spirituality—are so intimately connected that a presentation of one without the others is meaningless.[1] The issue of community,

---

1. The validity of a eucharistic celebration does not depend only on the presence of a validly ordained priest, who uses the correct matter (bread and wine) and who uses the correct words. To be valid a eucharistic celebration must take place within a Christian community. The presence of a Christian community constitutes

however, is the major basis for both eucharistic celebrations and eucharistic spirituality.

This book begins with the theme of community. On the basis of community, I then turn to the reality of the eucharistic celebration in the Roman Catholic Church. Only with an understanding of the basis of these two issues can one develop a eucharistic spirituality. The interconnection of community, Mass, and spirituality rests on four basic foundations, as follows:

1. The New Testament material for each of the three issues
2. The early church material for each of the same three issues
3. The major Western theological traditions as found from the twelfth to the sixteenth centuries
4. A eucharistic spirituality rooted in the above material but meaningful for Catholics who live in a post–Vatican II Church

These four basic areas appear and reappear as I weave together the interrelationship of community, Eucharist, and spirituality.

I want to thank a number of people who have made this book possible. First, I and American Catholics in general are grateful to The Catholic Community Foundation. I owe a particular debt of gratitude to Richard W. and Bernadette Miller, who have been the major leaders for the birth and development of The Catholic Community Foundation in Kansas City. The Millers' dream was profoundly encouraged by the bishop of Kansas City-St. Joseph, the Most Reverend Raymond J. Boland. Bishop Boland recognized the need for lay men and women to gain a more extensive and intensive part of today's Catholic Church. Despite health concerns, he attended all of the lecture series, and in his inimitable way he penned a special prayer for each of these days. I

---

a basis for the valid celebration of any eucharistic celebration. This volume does not attempt to prove this issue; such a proof is not the thesis of this book.

also want to express my gratitude to the son of Mr. and Mrs. Miller, Professor Richard W. Miller II, who worked beyond the limits of diligence to edit the three volumes that contain the lectures. I especially thank the editors of Liguori Publications for making all three volumes of this series available to a wider audience. In a special way, gratitude is due to the editorial staff at Liguori Publications: Editorial Director Hans Christoffersen and Acquisitions Editor Daniel Michaels. Because of their persistent help, I am able to present this expanded version of my own lecture. Needless to say, I owe much to my own religious community, the Franciscan Friars of the Saint Barbara Province, the western part of the United States. These men, over many years, have been a source of encouragement to me as a theology professor and as an author.

KENAN B. OSBORNE, OFM
FRANCISCAN SCHOOL OF THEOLOGY
GRADUATE THEOLOGICAL UNION
BERKELEY, CALIFORNIA

Chapter One

Christian Community

The basic theme of this volume is the following: the formation of a vibrant Christian community is the foundation and precondition for both the actual eucharistic celebration and a meaningful eucharistic spirituality. Unless the Christian community is striving to be a gospel community, both the celebrations of Eucharist and the efforts at a eucharistic spirituality will be essentially deficient. Jerome Murphy-O'Connor expresses this view straightforwardly: "There can be no eucharist in a community whose members do not love one another."[1]

The Contemporary Eucharistic Situation: Formulating the Contemporary Issue

This theme has a very practical application today. Attendance at weekend Mass has noticeably diminished in many Catholic churches of North America. Men and women who openly affirm that they are indeed Roman Catholics have found many excuses for not attending Sunday Mass. The literature on this subject is abundant. Diocesan bishops and local pastors have consistently raised the question, "What can we do to help our communities regain an enthusiasm for Sunday Mass?" In many

---

1. Jerome Murphy-O'Connor, "The First Letter to the Corinthians," in *The New Jerome Biblical Commentary,* eds. Raymond Brown, Joseph Fitzmyer, and Roland Murphy (Englewood Cliffs, NJ: Prentice Hall, 1990), 809.

1

dioceses, the bishops together with a committee of church leaders have developed a plan to encourage attendance throughout the diocese. The same is true at the parish level. Many pastors and parish councils have focused their efforts to reattract Catholic men and women to Sunday Mass. In the majority of instances, both the diocesan efforts and the parochial efforts usually have centered on the liturgy as a key point, if not *the* key point, for their programs. The thinking of these church leaders is that a more meaningful liturgy will result in better attendance at Sunday Mass.

Such a liturgical approach, however, can be questioned. Is liturgical improvement the correct central focus for such a renewal? Does a better liturgy provide a lasting foundation for continued attendance at Sunday Mass? In this chapter, I present several issues that argue against a centralizing liturgical focus. My argument indicates that liturgical improvement alone neither can nor should be considered the primary solution to non-attendance. Parishes in which liturgical changes have been made and the number of attendees has increased delight diocesan and parish leadership, but numbers alone do not indicate that parish life has become foundationally better. It is my contention that the formation of a gospel community is the better primary goal, since a more gospel-oriented community is the *sine qua non* foundation on which liturgy builds. Liturgical improvement has its place, but liturgy alone is neither the lasting key nor should it be the initial key, for the formation of diocesan or parochial Catholic communities. It is the community itself that needs to be enriched and deepened in its gospel-oriented qualities. The previous citation from Murphy-O'Connor sums up the situation crisply and accurately: there can be no Eucharist in a community whose members do not love one another.

The same position applies to the issue of spirituality. Some religious-minded leaders have attempted to develop a deeper eucharistic spirituality at either the parish or the diocesan level. These leaders have focused on an upgrading of eucharistic devotions, such as Benediction of the Blessed Sacrament and the recitation of the rosary before the tabernacle. Once again, one can legitimately ask, "Are liturgical and paraliturgical efforts the most effective way to achieve a eucharistic change in a diocese or parish community?" I argue that eucharistic devotions, though good in themselves, will have no lasting effect unless the community itself struggles to become a more gospel-oriented community. There can be no eucharistic devotion in a community whose members do not love one another.

My main issue, consequently, is that neither a strong liturgical renewal of Sunday eucharistic nor a more intense prayerful paraliturgical celebration of eucharistic devotions will have any lasting effect unless both of these liturgical renewals stem from a foundational renewal of the Christian community itself. What is unavoidably needed for the success of liturgical renewal is the pastoral development of a more vibrant gospel community at both the parish and the diocesan level. Parochial and diocesan leaders would be helped immensely if their initial endeavors did not center so strongly on liturgical renewal but rather focused more importantly on the development of a deeper communal spirit in the respective institutions.

An Outline of Our Journey

Accordingly, I consider some of the most important elements intrinsic to a deeper renewal of a Christian community *qua* community. This first chapter investigates the New Testament data on the Eucharist. Scriptural data are paramount for any such renewal, since no renewal of a Christian community can take place if the gospels, in particular, are not center stage to such a renewal.

The subsequent chapter considers historical eucharistic data from the early church period (100–600 CE). In many ways, what the first followers of Jesus did with regard to eucharistic theology has permanently shaped how succeeding Christian communities developed their own eucharistic celebrations. Moreover, early church data on the Eucharist were highly influential for the post–Vatican II renewal of eucharistic celebration. The liturgical and theological scholars who were selected for the post–Vatican II committees to renew the sacramental ritual of the Eucharist were well versed in early church eucharistic data, and the renewed rituals for the individual sacraments that they eventually developed reflect this early church influence.

In the third chapter, on the basis of the New Testament and the early church material, I briefly consider the major theological developments that took place from the twelfth to the sixteenth centuries. Without any doubt, this theological material requires volumes to do it justice. A small volume such as this one can only highlight the major theological issues of both the scholastic period and the Tridentine period. The scholastic period engendered a *renewal in the theology of the Eucharist*. The Tridentine period engendered a *renewal of the institutional celebration of the Eucharist*. Both of these eucharistic renewals, the theological and the institutional, affected the Roman Catholic Church for the next four hundred years. Catholics living in the twenty-first century cannot minimize this eucharistic scholastic-Tridentine tradition. An eight-hundred–year tradition is formidable. Nonetheless, it is also vulnerable. From the last decades of the nineteenth century and throughout the entire twentieth century, the eucharistic scholastic-Tridentine tradition has undergone slow and subtle changes. The chapters on the scholastic-Tridentine Eucharist and its aftermath are, consequently, an important bridge for the basic thesis of this book.

The final chapter considers in some detail two major issues affecting today's Christian communities, their celebration of the Mass, and their eucharistic spirituality. These two issues are (1) the Eucharist and its relationship to the word of God and (2) the Eucharist of the world and the Eucharist of the altar.

In the post–Vatican II period of Church life, many problems

4

confront today's Christian communities. No generic Christian community exists that can be cloned from one community to another. Neither in all of Christian history has there been an idyllic Christian community that can serve as the paragon image for all other Christian communities. There are and have been from the beginning of Christianity only actually existing Christian communities. Each of these Christian communities has had to face its own problematic areas, just as we today must face our own problematic time with regard to our own actually existing Christian communities.

Community and Eucharist in the New Testament

From the beginnings of the Jesus community in the first century until the present day, Christian theology and Christian tradition have held, in some way or another, to the position that every eucharistic celebration is based on the actual presence of a Christian community. The reality of an existential Christian community and the reality of an existential eucharistic celebration have been untiringly united throughout the history of the Christian world. The bishops at Vatican II expressed this connection of liturgy and community in a very clear way: "Liturgical services are not private functions but are celebrations of the Church which is the 'sacrament of unity.'"[2]

The New Testament passages on Eucharist unanimously join the two issues: a strong gospel-oriented Christian community on the one hand, and on the other a prayerful eucharistic celebration by the community. The New Testament's portrayal of the first postresurrection-Jesus communities provides us today with some general guidelines for the development of our own

---

2. Vatican II: The Constitution on the Sacred Liturgy (*Sacrosanctum Concilium*), December 4, 1963, 26.

Christian communities. The New Testament data are reviewed in the following order:

1. Paul's presentation of Eucharist
2. The synoptics' presentation of Eucharist
3. John's presentation of Eucharist

The Eucharist in the Writings of Paul

Chronologically, the first New Testament writer who focused on the theme of Eucharist was Saint Paul. His First Letter to the Corinthians is generally dated around 53–54 CE.[3] The dating of this letter is significant, since it was written roughly twentysome years after the resurrection event and about fifteen years before the first gospel was written. As such, Paul's statements are the first extant written materials on Eucharist that the Christian churches have. His major references to Eucharist are in chapters 10 and 11 of the First Letter to the Corinthians.

From the very start of his letter, Paul was concerned about the Jesus quality of the Corinthian community. From verses 1:10 to 4:21, Paul describes the rival groups in the community, and the presence of such rival groups is not, in Paul's view, Christ-centered. From verses 5:1 to 6:20, Paul focuses on two particularly divisive issues: the sexual behavior of some community members and the lawsuits filed in pagan courts by other community members. Shortly before Paul wrote his first letter to the Corinthians, he had received a written communication from the Corinthian community asking for help on certain defined questions. From verses 7:1 to 14:40, Paul responds to these particular questions. It is in this section that we find the two chapters on the Eucharist.

---

3. Cf. Murphy-O'Connor, ibid. 799. From the time of Jesus' death (c. 30 CE) down to 54 CE, we have no written data. Some biblical scholars refer to this twenty-four–year period as the scriptural "black hole." Any statement describing what took place in these twenty-four years is, at best, conjectural.

In chapter 10, Paul begins by emphasizing the community itself. Notice that Paul speaks of the community before he turns to the actual celebration of Eucharist. For Paul, the spiritual health of the community is the *sine qua non* foundation for any eucharistic celebration. In Paul's view, the Corinthian community is neither a community that is cohesive in itself around Christ nor is it a community that reflects the coming of the Lord. If the community does not reflect the Lord, how can there be a genuine eucharistic celebration? On the basis of his argument for a more Christ-centered community, Paul, in chapter 11, turns to the eucharistic celebration at Corinth. It is evident in the construction of the letter itself that Paul makes an essential interrelationship between community and Eucharist. His insistence on this essential interrelationship needs further consideration. Let us examine the contents of his letter more closely.

Paul was not in Corinth when he wrote his letter; rather, he was in Ephesus, which was a major port city of Asia Minor (present-day Turkey). As mentioned previously, Paul had received a letter from the Corinthian community (7:1) in which a number of troublesome issues were raised. Prior to writing his letter, Paul had also been advised in person regarding some additional critical issues that some friends of an Ephesian businesswoman, named Chloe, had related to him. These friends of Chloe had recently returned from Corinth to Ephesus and had provided Paul with an oral accounting of certain practices in the Corinthian community that they had found questionable. One of the issues Chloe's friends had mentioned was the Corinthian celebration of Eucharist. In chapter 11, Paul centers on the abuses regarding the Corinthian celebration of Eucharist as presented to him. We read the following:

> *Now in the following instructions I do not commend you, because when you come together it is not for the better but for the worse. For, to begin with, when you*

come together as a church,[4] *I hear that there are divisions among you; and to some extent I believe it. Indeed, there have to be factions among you, for only so will it become clear who among you are genuine. When you come together, it is not really to eat the Lord's supper. For when the time comes to eat, each of you goes ahead with your own supper, and one goes hungry and another becomes drunk. What! Do you not have homes to eat and drink in? Or do you show contempt for the church of God and humiliate those who have nothing? What should I say to you? Should I commend you? In this matter I do not commend you!* (1 Corinthians 11:17–22).

Murphy-O'Connor has centered much of his research on Paul's letters to the Corinthians. In 1983, he published *St. Paul's Corinth: Texts and Archaeology.*[5] In this book, Murphy-O'Connor presents the results of his archeological studies on Corinthian dining rooms that existed in the first century CE. He measured several dining areas in the neighborhood of Corinth and described them in detail. The dining area for a fairly wealthy family was generally a room in which one of the four walls was actually an open space through which one could see an outside atrium or patio. Thus, people in the outside atrium could observe what was going on at the meal that was taking place inside.

For the meal, the people inside reclined on built-in benches connected to one of the three interior walls. Reclining at table for a meal was the accepted practice in the Hellenistic world. The benches at the back wall were for the host or owner of the house, his relatives, and/or his most respected guests. The

---

4. The Greek phrase here is εν εκκλησια—"in a gathering." This likely would be what liturgical authors today call a "house-church" or a "house-place for gathering together." In Paul's time, the Jesus community did not own a church building such as we have today.

5. Murphy-O'Connor, *St. Paul's Corinth: Texts and Archaeology*, ed 3 rev. (Collegeville, MN: Liturgical Press, 2002).

benches along the two side walls were for the other guests, but in an order of social ranking. The more respected guests were closer to the back wall, and the less respected guests were closer to the wall that opened out to the patio.

The central section of the dining room was an open area, allowing the servants to enter and exit to bring and serve food or to furnish other necessary items. In front of each reclining guest was a small table on which the food and drink were placed. Naturally, the people in these dining rooms tended to be the more wealthy guests, whereas those in the atrium were the less fortunate.

> The [eucharistic] meal was celebrated in a private house whose rooms were too small to contain the whole community in one area. The division thus imposed may have been exacerbated by the Roman custom of classifying guests socially and giving little or nothing to those considered inferior.[6]

In measuring the Corinthian dining rooms, Murphy-O'Connor was able to determine the number of privileged guests who could physically share a meal in such a dining area. A small dining room could accommodate nine guests: at the back wall would be a bench for the host and two benches for his family or special guests. Along the two side walls there would be three benches each, accommodating a total of six guests. In all, nine people would enjoy a banquet. All others remained in the open patio or atrium area.

With this illustration in mind we can understand Paul's complaint. At a eucharistic gathering, which would have included a meal, the host and his special friends were well plied with food and drink, while those who were not special friends remained

---

6. Murphy-O'Connor, "The First Letter to the Corinthians," 809. Also see *St. Paul's Corinth*: 178–91.

in the open area with little to nothing either to eat or to drink. The very structure of the dining room prevented a community meal. Rather, it divided the community, and it is precisely the lack of a community that is at the center of Paul's complaint against the Corinthians. A eucharistic community cannot be a true gathering in which there are the "haves" and the "have nots." In other words, Paul, in his complaint, clearly states that a Jesus community itself is the necessary basis for any and every celebration of the Eucharist, not vice versa. A genuine Eucharist cannot involve only a few people who communally celebrate the eucharistic meal while the majority are present basically as on-lookers. Once again, we must acknowledge Murphy-O'Connor's strong warning:

> The essence of his [Paul's] reaction is that there can be no eucharist in a community whose members do not love one another.[7]

After expressing his complaint about the Corinthian eucharistic meal, Paul expresses the basis for his own eucharistic theology. This basis is the tradition that he had come to know regarding the Lord's supper.

In an essay first written by C. P. M. Jones and then revised by C. J. A. Hickling, we hear the same message just described. These authors write:

> We are now in a position to sketch out the rite of the Lord's Supper as Paul had introduced it in Corinth and as he wished it to be maintained. It is a plenary session and should not begin until all are assembled. It is a real meal, to which the well-off contribute food and drink. It opens with the customary Jewish blessing of God over the bread which is then broken in pieces and distributed

---

7. Ibid., 809.

to all, probably with words of interpretation or distri-
bution identifying the bread as the Body of Christ. By
this gathering it is constituted as the ecclesial Body of
Christ.[8]

For Paul, such a communal meal celebrated by followers of Jesus
has only one foundation: Jesus himself. For Paul, a vibrant Jesus
community is the essential element for any and every communal
Christian celebration of Eucharist. He writes:

*For I received from the Lord what I also handed on
to you, that the Lord Jesus on the night when he was
betrayed took a loaf of bread, and when he had given
thanks, he broke it and said: "This is my body that is for
you. Do this in remembrance of me." In the same way
he took the cup also, after supper, saying, "This cup is
the new covenant in my blood. Do this, as often as you
drink it, in remembrance of me." For as often as you eat
this bread and drink the cup, you proclaim the Lord's
death until he comes* (1 Corinthians 11:23–26).

In this Pauline passage, the author uses the word *you* many
times, but it is never singular; it is always plural. This is clearly
evident in the Greek text of Paul's letter. The Greek word is
consistently "υμεις" (the plural for "you") and not "συ" (the
singular for "you"). Paul is addressing his words to a group (the
disciples) and not merely to an individual. This interpretation is
substantiated by Paul's opening remarks in which he says that
his letter is addressed "to the church of God that is in Corinth"
(1 Corinthians 1:2). Throughout his letter, Paul continually
addresses the community. He does so regarding a community

8. C. P. M. Jones revised by C. J. A. Hickling, "The Eucharist: The New
Testament," in *The Study of Liturgy*, eds. Cheslyn Jones, Geoffrey Wainwright,
Edward Yarnold, and Paul Bradshaw (London: Oxford University Press,
1992), 192–93.

that has become deeply split by internal division (see 1 Corinthians 1:10–4:21).[9] His focus on community can be seen in the section of his letter regarding the issue of the Jesus community taking their altercations to non-Christian judges (see 1 Corinthians 6:1–11). He chastises the Corinthians for not being a gospel community, since their immoral behavior of fornication and idolatry contradicts the ethical goals of Jesus himself (see Corinthians 8:1–11:1). As a counterweight to such division and lack of Christian integrity, in chapter 11 Paul presents one of his most important statements on the Eucharist as a communal celebration.

Unity with Jesus by the community is Paul's urgent call, since Jesus in the Eucharist wants to be united to the community. The first extant writing that the Christian church can claim focuses strongly on the unity of Jesus with a community of his followers as they celebrate the Eucharist. However, for Paul there is more than just a union between Eucharist and community. Paul insists that the foundation of Eucharist is a gospel-oriented community. Without a gospel-oriented community, the validity of Eucharist is diminished.

In another essay entitled "Eucharist and Community in First Corinthians," Murphy-O'Connor does not focus on the physical aspects of the dining area and its patio or atrium but on the quality of the community itself.[10] His basis for this emphasis is on Jesus himself, namely, "For I received from the Lord what I also handed on to you" (11:23). Paul had conveyed Jesus' own instruction to the Corinthians themselves. He had explained to

---

9. In 1 Corinthians 1:2, the Greek text reads "τη εκκλησια του Θεου τη ουση εν Κορινθω." The phrase "church of God" refers to the Corinthian community of Jesus itself. It does not refer to any hierarchical leaders of this Jesus community, nor does it refer to an architectural form of church present in Corinth.

10. Murphy-O'Connor, "Eucharist and Community in First Corinthians," in *Living Bread, Saving Cup*, ed. R. Kevin Seaoltz (Collegeville, MN: Liturgical Press, 1982), 1–29.

the Corinthian community what had happened at the Lord's supper itself. Joseph Fitzmyer explains Paul's understanding as follows:

> For Paul the eucharist is above all the "Lord's Supper," the repast at which the new people of God eats its "spiritual food" and consumes its "spiritual drink." In this act it manifests itself as the community of the "new covenant," as it shares in "the table of the Lord." The communion of this people denotes not only its union with Christ and with one another, but also a proclamation of the Christ-event and its eschatological character.[11]

Fitzmyer's use of *community* is noteworthy. The Eucharist "manifests" the Christian community, and the community "denotes" the Christ event and the resurrection event. The community, in this presentation, underlies the eucharistic celebration. The two issues are united: community *and* Eucharist, but in this citation, it is the community that is the foundation for the Eucharist, not vice versa.

In the conclusion of his own essay, Murphy-O'Connor explains in some detail Paul's eucharistic understanding on this matter. He writes:

> The dominant characteristic of Paul's treatment of the Eucharist is its extreme realism. There is no exalted poetry, no flights into mysticism. It is firmly rooted in his concept of the community of faith as the basic reality of the New Age introduced by the death of Christ.[12]

---

11. Joseph Fitzmyer, "Pauline Theology," *The New Jerome Biblical Commentary*: 1411.

12. Murphy-O'Connor, "Eucharist and Community in First Corinthians," 1–29.

Murphy-O'Connor then describes Paul's view of the community of faith. "Christ remains incarnationally present in and to the world through the community that is his body."[13] "The person of Christ is really present under the sacramental species only when the words of institution are spoken by 'Christ,' [namely] an authentic community animated by the creative saving love which alone enables humanity to 'live.'"[14]

Paul's reaction to the actual and existential eucharistic celebration in Corinth was negative and critical. In Paul's view, the celebration was deficient because there was no evidence of a solid and profound eucharistic Christian *community*. He therefore took the Corinthians to task not on the basis of their celebration of Eucharist, but on their lack of a credible Christian community. Paul's focus on the community of faith is not simply an issue of interrelationality. Paul indicates, in no uncertain terms, that the Christian community of faith in the Corinthian gathering is the necessary and most essential reality. It is the foundation and basis for eucharistic celebration. Paul's complaint is primarily focused on their totally inadequate community of faith. Only when there is an adequate community of faith can there be a true eucharistic celebration of the Lord's supper, and only on the basis of these two can we speak of a *eucharistic spirituality*. In his commentary of 1 Corinthians, Murphy-O'Connor is even more explicit: "Even though the ritual words (1 Corinthians 11:24–25) were said, the lack of love (1 Corinthians 11:21–22) meant that in reality there was no eucharist."[15]

What does a community of faith signify? Paul, in his Letters to the Corinthians, specifies that an ideal community of faith entails these preconditions: (1) the community is one, (2) the community is Christ, and (3) the community is alive in Christ. Each of these is detailed in the following text.

---

13. Ibid., 6.
14. Ibid., 30.
15. Ibid., "The First Letter to the Corinthians," 809.

The Community Is One

The term *body of Christ* too often focuses on the different parts of a body, and by application, to various parts of the Christian church. Murphy-O'Connor states that Paul focuses more on the organic unity of the body image. He writes:

> We think of individuals coming together to create community. For Paul it is precisely the reverse. The community is a radically new reality (1 Corinthians 1:28) which makes the believer a new creation (2 Corinthians 5:17). We consider unity as something to be created, whereas Paul saw this unity as primary and envisaged individuals as being changed by absorption into that unity.[16]

Following this line of thought, the community is foundational; the individual is changed by his or her entry into such a community. As a consequence, the community is foundational for the celebration of Eucharist. We hear today that the Eucharist makes the Church and the Church makes the Eucharist. Paul might not agree with this axiom. A truly gospel community is needed before an individual is changed and before these changed individuals celebrate the Eucharist. Conversely, a divided community—one in which the leaders eat and drink in abundance while the remaining members have little to nothing—is an affront to a Jesus community. Community and Eucharist are essentially intertwined, but community is the more foundational.

An intensified need exists for a unified Christian community in today's Church. The sexual-abuse crisis of the clergy and the overall public perception of the American bishops' failure of moral authority have produced many disunified dioceses and parishes. Add to this the continuing division of Catholics over the changes that followed Vatican II. In every postconciliar time there has generally been a lengthy disunity of Catholic life, and

---

16. Ibid., "Eucharistic Community in First Corinthians," 5.

Vatican II is no exception to this tension between conciliar acceptance and conciliar rejection.

A diocesan or parish goal of renewing the liturgy will be ineffective if a loving and unified community is not understood as the quintessential basis for any and all good liturgy. Thus, the diocesan and pastoral priorities should clearly urge a more unified community over all other goals. Diocesan and parish leadership alike should ask the question: "Is one's diocesan/parish community unified and mutually loving, or is it disunified and factious?" If disunified and factious, Paul would render a similar judgment on today's dioceses and parishes as he did on the Corinthian community: "I hear that when you meet as a church, there are divisions among you."

The same situation applies to contemporary religious communities of both men and women. When these religious communities celebrate Eucharist, is there unity or disunity among the members? Religious communities must ask themselves whether the words of Paul have any application to their own situation: "I hear that when you meet as a church, there are divisions among you."

Paul clearly unites community and Eucharist, but they are interrelated in a way that emphasizes the need of community first, since a unified community is the requisite basis for Eucharist. A disunified community distorts the very reality of Eucharist. It should also be noted that for Paul a Christian community does not mean a unified institution. Christian unity does not mean, today, conformity to the institutional hierarchy. The center for Paul is Jesus. Jesus determines the community; a community does not determine who Jesus is or what Jesus means. Christology determines ecclesiology; ecclesiology does not determine Christology. Unity, therefore, in today's parishes and dioceses is not a rigid conformity to hierarchy. Hierarchy has its place, of course. As a community, the hierarchy itself needs to be a Jesus community. If it is simply its own institution, it is clearly neither Jesus-based nor Jesus-oriented. Developing a gospel community—a Jesus community—should be the goal of both the parish and the diocese, since the gospel or Jesus unifies a Christian community in its most fundamental depths.

The Community Is Christ

A second issue is Christological. For Paul, the community is the "incarnational prolongation of the mission of the saving Christ. What he did in and for the world of his day through his physical presence, the community does in and for its world."[17] By entering the community, which is Christ, through faith and baptism, believers are absorbed into the organic unity that is "one man."[18]

Again, one can see that if a Jesus community is not unified in its understanding of Jesus, it will not be a Christian community even when it attempts to celebrate a Eucharist. Today, we need to ask about our own situation. How deeply Jesus-oriented is our parish community? Our diocesan community? Our religious community? If the celebration of Eucharist in any of these communities suffers from a certain form of inertia, the major issue cannot be a focus on making the liturgy more exciting. Rather, it should be focused on making Jesus more exciting. Liturgical renewal might indeed be needed, but a Jesus renewal is a far more fundamental need for such communities.

The Community Is Alive in Christ

The third precondition for the ideal faith community involves its ongoing efforts. If the community strives to be what God intended it to be, then and only then will the community be *alive* in Christ. Sin, unfortunately, exists in every community. A major symptom of a sinful community is disunity, and disunity means that a community is neither Christ nor alive in Christ. Paul goes on to indicate that sin is often brought about

17. Ibid., 6.
18. Ibid., 7.

through the manipulation of the community by its leaders who act in ways that are contrary to the goal of living in Christ. Paul writes:

> *Whoever, therefore, eats the bread or drinks the cup of the Lord in an unworthy manner will be answerable for the body and blood of the Lord. Examine yourselves, and only then eat of the bread and drink of the cup. For all who eat and drink without discerning the body, eat and drink judgment against themselves. For this reason many of you are weak and ill, and some have died. But if we judged ourselves, we would not be judged. But when we are judged by the Lord, we are disciplined so that we may not be condemned along with the world.*
>
> *So then, my brothers and sisters, when you come together to eat, wait for one another. If you are hungry, eat at home, so that when you come together, it will not be for your condemnation* (1 Corinthians 11:27–33).

Structures, endorsed by the leadership and countenanced by the community itself, are often the major areas of sinfulness in a community. It is not only the individual who is the sinner and who thereby compromises the community. Rather, it is the community structure itself, endorsed and manipulated both by the leadership and by the quiet acquiescence of others, that creates the sinfulness of a community. Hostile divisions were taken for granted by the Corinthians; jealousy and strife had become a habitual pattern of their life. Paul centers on these kinds of issues that are evident in the Corinthian community, and his inexorable emphasis on community indicates to us that a Jesus community is the basis of all true Christian reality, including the reality of Eucharist.

Not only is it the mode of existence willed by the Creator, but it is the only practical concrete means whereby an individual is rescued from the false orientation of a fallen world. Only in an authentically Christian community is the individual free to be as God intended.[19]

Freedom for men and women is not an individual thing. It is rather a quality of community that benefits one another. Without a Jesus community committed to living Christian values, there is no genuine freedom.[20] In First Corinthians the leadership of the Jesus community holds a Eucharist in which those who are wealthy eat well, while those who are poor are snubbed. There is no unity, no Christ as community, no life in Christ in such a community. In such a community, there is structural sin manipulated by those who are important, and there is, as a consequence, an absence of freedom in Christ.

The portrayal by Paul (to come to the Eucharist in a worthy manner, and to wait for one another) is a description of an ideal community. It is an ideal faith community in which the Eucharist is genuinely *celebrated* and from which eucharistic spirituality emerges. Unfortunately, most Christian communities are not ideal, and thus there is in most Christian communities structural sin, individual sin, and a structural lack of freedom. In precisely these three areas—structural sin, individual sin, and a structural lack of freedom—a Christian community today should examine itself in depth. These three areas need to be seen as the first priorities of community renewal. The priority should not focus on liturgical issues, even though these might also need a renewal. The priority should not focus on canonical issues, even though these, too, might need a renewal.

On the basis of the above material from Paul, let us turn to the next group of Christian writers, namely, Mark, Matthew, and Luke.

---

19. Ibid., 13.
20. Ibid., 12–14.

The Eucharist in the Writings
of the Synoptic Gospels

The synoptic gospels, written several years after Paul's death, also witness to the unity of community and Eucharist. None of the synoptic gospels indicates that the authors were acquainted with the letters of Paul. Most scholars today conclude that the three synoptic gospels were written after the destruction of the Temple in 70 CE but before the mid- to later 90s CE.[21] Many scholars have evaluated and interpreted the gospel passages on the Eucharist. Some have noted that such a task is delicate and difficult, since the evidence is slender and fragmentary. A. H. Courtain goes so far as to say that "what the New Testament writings presuppose...is of greater importance than what they actually describe."[22]

By the time the authors of the synoptic gospels wrote their respective works, the Jesus communities had already developed some rudimentary liturgical wordings for their eucharistic celebration. These earliest liturgical wordings would not have been as standardized and centrally regulated as are the liturgical texts in use today. Moreover, the Eucharist at this early date remained a part of an evening meal, celebrated by a Jesus community in the context of a home. As a result, one can argue cautiously that the various New Testament texts regarding the Lord's supper reflect in small ways some of the liturgical language used by differing local communities around 70 to 85 CE. However, it cannot be said with any surety that the synoptic wording over the bread and wine was the exact wording of Jesus himself at the supper before his death. After

---

21. One of several authors who date Mark's Gospel prior to the destruction of the Temple is Daniel Harrington, "The Gospel According to Mark," *The New Jerome Biblical Commentary*, 597.

22. A. H. Courtain, "The Sacrifice of Praise," *Theology* 58 (August 1955): 290.

the resurrection event, the disciples recalled his words but added interpretative details to them.[23]

The eucharistic gospel passages as found in Mark, Matthew, and Luke likewise reflect interpretations of the Jesus event itself, which the communities of Mark, Matthew, and Luke had developed. In other words, these authors and their communities saw the following in the Eucharist's connection to the Jesus event:

- A relationship to Jesus' earlier meals in which he participated daily with his disciples, with tax collectors, with Mary and Martha, and so on (a look backward, *anamnesis*).
- A relationship to the future eschatological banquet of the Lord in the risen life (a look forward, *prolepsis*).

From the language used by the gospel authors, we notice words that involve a memory of Jesus (*anamnesis*); words that have a present meaning such as "Take and eat" (*existential*); and words that involve the resurrection, such as drinking anew in the kingdom of God (*prolepsis*). This triadic relationship clearly indicates that the earliest postresurrection followers of Jesus had to some extent theologized on the meaning of the overarching Jesus event and interpreted a eucharistic celebration as a triadic relationship to the Jesus event.

Nonetheless, one must be careful about generalized statements regarding these early eucharistic liturgies and interpretations. From the gospel passages cited below we can only conclude that what each of the evangelists has written in his own gospel evidences to some extant incipient liturgical formulations. Such a caution does not, however, minimize the gospel passages on the Last Supper. Rather, we do hear in these gospel passages faint

---

23. Some scholars tend to generalize in an undue way the synoptic material on Eucharist. One must be careful not to overgeneralize the data. One cannot conclude, for instance, that in this period of time "all the communities" did the same thing as recorded in the gospels.

but important indications of the actual eucharistic celebrations in the respective communities of these authors.[24]

Let us consider each synoptic gospel and its eucharistic statements. These are found in their individual gospels' recounting of the Last Supper. We begin with Mark, who is generally recognized as the first author of a synoptic gospel.

The Gospel of Mark

While they were eating, he took a loaf of bread, and after blessing it he broke it, gave it to them, and said, "Take; this is my body." Then he took a cup, and after giving thanks he gave it to them, and all of them drank from it. He said to them, "This is my blood of the covenant, which is poured out for many. Truly I tell you, I will never again drink of the fruit of the vine until that day when I drink it new in the kingdom of God" (Mark 14:22–25).

In these words of Mark, we see that Jesus is not talking to individuals but his community of the Twelve (see 14:17). It was during a communal meal, celebrated by Jesus and the Twelve, that bread and wine became the eucharistic symbols of Jesus' own body and blood. Mark is writing about a past event, but he also witnesses at least indirectly that the Markan community itself had continued in some form or another to celebrate a memorial meal of the Last Supper. In Mark's account, we find key aspects of the community's theological interpretation of the eucharistic meal, such as the belief that the Eucharist is both a sacred memorial and a communal meal. Mention is made of a remembrance (*anamnesis*) of the Jesus covenant, of the grace that the suffering and death brought to many, including the

---

24. Cf. Salvatore Marsili, "Teologia della celebrazione dell'eucaristia," *La Liturgia, Eucaristica: telogia e storia della celebrazione* (Genoa: Casa Editrice Marietti, 1983), 11–12.

Markan community itself (*existential*), and of the relationship of the meal not only to the death of Jesus but to the risen Jesus in the heavenly kingdom of God (*prolepsis*). The following terms are the indications of their theological interpretation: "while they were eating" (eucharistic meal and a community); "after the blessing" (eucharist = ευλογησας = to bless); "blood of the covenant" (a new covenant); "poured out for many" (salvific grace); and "until that day when I drink it new in the kingdom of God" (risen life = eschatology). The theological interpretations behind these issues are not spelled out in the Markan text; rather, they are liturgically, and therefore indirectly, highlighted by the Markan community in its own celebration of a meal.

One phrase in this section of Mark's Gospel deserves special mention, namely, Jesus "took some bread, and when he had said the *blessing* he broke it and gave it to them." The phrase "he said the blessing"—in Greek, ευλογησας—translates the Hebrew *berekah*. Another Greek word, which often translated the Hebrew word *berekah*, is Eucharist—in Greek ευχαριστειν. The *berekah* was a blessing that Jewish families used at the beginning and ending of family meals. For the ordinary meals of a workweek, the *berekah* was said in a brief and straightforward way. For the weekly Sabbath meal, the wording of the *berekah* involved a more elaborate formulation. For very special days, such as Passover, there were intricate forms for the *berekah*.

In the middle of the twentieth century, liturgical scholars in Europe and North America researched how the early followers of Jesus used the Jewish *berekah* as part of their own communal celebrations of the eucharistic meal. These scholars pointed out that the earliest eucharistic prayers followed the structural pattern of the Jewish *berekah*.[25] This relationship of Christian

---

25. See Joachim Jeremias, *Eucharistic Words of Jesus* (London, SCM, 1966); Gregory Dix, *The Shape of the Liturgy* (New York: Seabury, 1982); David Daube, *He That Cometh* (London: Diocesan Council for Jewish-Christian Understanding, 1966); and *Wine in the Bible* (London: Diocesan Council for Jewish-Christian Understanding, 1974).

Eucharist to Jewish *berekah* helps us to see more clearly the relationship of a Christian Eucharist to a community. The *berekah* was a communal prayer; so, too, the Eucharist is a communal prayer. In both situations, the community is the foundation for the meal itself, for the *berekah* and for the eucharistic prayer.

For Mark and his community, it was the gathering of the Jesus community itself that made the celebration of the eucharistic meal a reality. Without the community, there would have been no eucharistic celebration at all. For Mark, a single individual celebrating the eucharistic meal would have been unthinkable. A community celebrates a meal. An individual eats alone.

The Gospel of Matthew

We move to the Gospel of Matthew, who lived in a different locale than Mark and who shared in a Jesus community that theologically moved in a distinct way compared with the theological centering of the Markan Gospel. When Matthew turns his attention to the Lord's supper, he writes:

> *While they were eating, Jesus took a loaf of bread and after blessing it he broke it, gave it to the disciples, and said, "Take, eat; this is my body." Then he took a cup, and after giving thanks he gave it to them, saying, "Drink from it, all of you; for this is my blood of the covenant, which is poured out for many for the forgiveness of sins. I tell you, I will never again drink of this fruit of the vine until that day when I drink it new with you in my Father's kingdom"* (Matthew 26:26–29).

When Matthew was writing his Gospel, as many scholars have shown, he had before him a copy of the Gospel of Mark. Matthew follows the sequencing of events in the Gospel of Mark but changes the sequence on a number of occasions.[26] His description of the Last Supper closely resembles that of Mark. Matthew even uses similar terminology: "covenant," "for many," "I shall not drink," and so on. Even the words over the bread and wine are basically the same in Matthew as those found in Mark. In Matthew, mention is made of *disciples*—μαθηται—rather than the Twelve. In 26:17–19, Matthew had already mentioned the disciples, who had asked about the preparation for the Passover, and Jesus had instructed them on how to make the preparations. The disciples had then followed out Jesus' instructions.[27] In the Matthaean passage cited above, however, we read: "[Jesus] took his place with the twelve" (26:20). One might ask: Where are the other disciples who prepared the Passover meal? Perhaps this lack of clarity is merely textual. Not only does the presence of these other disciples in Matthew's Gospel at the supper raise the issue regarding the number of people at the Last Supper, but also there are other indications that Jesus and the Twelve were not the only ones at this supper.

The repetition of such words and phrases as "covenant," "took the bread," and "said certain words" provides a small insight into the way in which the Jesus community of Matthew's locale celebrated a communal eucharistic service. This community took pains to preserve the insights of Jesus' own Last Supper, and this preservation of words and phrases indicates to us how they interpreted the eucharistic communal celebration. Their Eucharist was seen as a memorial, a communal meal, and a foretaste of

---

26. In Matthew's Gospel, from 3:1 to 4:22 there is no change in order from Mark's order; from 4:23 to 13:58 there are five changes in the Markan order; from 14:1 to the end there are no changes in order from Mark.

27. Robert Karris, "The Gospel According to Luke," *The New Jerome Biblical Commentary*, 715. If the disciples in 24:27–29 were not part of the Twelve and if they had prepared the Passover, then there were certainly more in attendance at the Last Supper than simply Jesus and the Twelve. Since the Reformation the leadership of the Church has stressed the presence of only the Twelve, and they did so for apologetic reasons rather than exegetical reasons.

the heavenly meal with Jesus in the Father's kingdom—risen life. Matthew, too, uses the Greek word ευχαριστησας = eucharist, which translates as *berekah* in Hebrew. The connection between early New Testament celebration and the Jewish blessing at a communal meal is once again apparent.

In the text of Matthew, Jesus enjoins the disciples to eat and to drink, and he does this in a stronger way than Mark had done. In this strengthening of these phrases, it is evident that Matthew is giving an approbation to the community's liturgical celebration of the supper. Although wording might be important, since it provides clues to liturgical interpretations, Xavier Léon-Dufour states that the supper is primarily an action, not a recitation. What Jesus and the disciples did, as well as what the early Jesus community itself is doing, is far more important than the words.[28]

> Two main actions are described, one concerned with the bread, the other concerned with the cup. Each action is presented as a totality, but is made up of various gestures.[29]

In today's eucharistic ritual, there is a tendency from the beginning of Mass until its end to talk and talk and talk. Liturgy, however, is ritual. It is action. Somehow, the new post–Vatican II eucharistic ritual is more verbal than action-centered. A Jesus community is not simply a community that thinks alike. It is an action-oriented community, not an ideology-oriented community. In other words, the eucharistic community *strives* (action) to be Christlike, *follows* (action) the impulse of the Holy Spirit, and leaves the table (action) to bring the meaning of Eucharist

---

28. Xavier Léon-Dufour, *Sharing the Eucharistic Bread: The Witness of the New Testament*, trans. Matthew O'Connell (New York: Paulist Press, 1987), 50–69.

29. Ibid., 51.

to daily life. A eucharistic liturgy that is more talkative than active, more catechetical than practical, and more ideological and dogmatic than personal and existential is a defective celebration of eucharistic action. But this action orientation is also the major characteristic of a Jesus community: there can be no Eucharist in a community whose members do not love one another.

The Gospel of Luke

Let us consider the data from the Gospel of Luke. Where and when Luke wrote his Gospel has been an issue of argument for many centuries. Generally, scholars establish the time of writing as after the writing of Mark's Gospel and to some degree around the same time as the writing of Matthew's Gospel. The actual place of the writing is variously presented, but the large city of Syrian Antioch seems to be the favored locale. Luke, as did Matthew, had in front of him a copy of Mark's Gospel. However, he does not seem to know anything about the Gospel of Matthew. Luke borrows material from Mark, but not in a slavish way nor as extensively as Matthew does. Luke's sequencing is quite different from that of Mark and Matthew, and he includes material that neither Mark nor Matthew present. Consequently, when we read the Gospel of Luke, we are clearly in a different locale than those of either Mark or Matthew. In the Lukan Gospel we hear a belief in the Eucharist that reflects a different Jesus community than those reflected in either Mark or Matthew.

The theological understanding of Eucharist in Luke has some emphases that are lacking in both Mark and Matthew. In other words, we hear the voices of a different existential community, struggling to fulfill the teaching of Jesus. However, as G. B. Caird once wrote: "The Lukan account of the Last Supper is a scholar's paradise and a beginner's nightmare."[30]

---

30. G. B. Caird, *Saint Luke* (New York: Penguin, 1963), 237.

When the hour came, he took his place at the table, and the apostles with him. He said to them, "I have eagerly desired to eat this Passover with you before I suffer; for I tell you, I will not eat it until it is fulfilled in the kingdom of God." Then he took a cup, and after giving thanks he said, "Take this and divide it among yourselves; for I tell you that from now on I will not drink of the fruit of the vine until the kingdom of God comes." Then he took a loaf of bread, and when he had given thanks, he broke it and gave it to them, saying, "This is my body, which is given for you. Do this in remembrance of me." And he did the same with the cup after supper, saying, "This cup that is poured out for you is the new covenant in my blood" (Luke 22:14–20).

In this Lukan passage on the Last Supper, the presentation is in many ways quite different from either Mark or Matthew. Luke places the blessing of the cup first, that is, at the beginning of the meal, and then he adds a second blessing of the cup at the end of the Passover meal. In Luke, the context of a Passover meal is clear, and for the Jewish people at the time of Jesus, a Passover meal was the major communal celebration of the entire year. Robert Karris, however, reminds us:

> The common designation of this meal as the "Last Supper" should not blind readers of Luke's Gospel to the fact that this is the last meal in a long series of meals in which Jesus, "the glutton and drunkard, friend of toll collectors and sinners" (7:34) has been involved (see 5:27–32; 7:31–34; 15:1–2; 19:7). This meal Jesus shares with his apostles and disciples, who also are sinners in need of forgiveness, mercy, and protection.[31]

---

31. See Karris, op. cit., 715.

In ways similar to those in the gospels of Mark and Matthew, we see that in Luke's Gospel, community and Eucharist are intimately conjoined. Without a community, no Passover meal would have been celebrated; without a community, no Last Supper and no later communal Eucharists would have been celebrated.

In Luke, the interconnection of community and Eucharist is a given. Paul, as we have seen, clearly argued that a gospel-oriented community is a necessary prerequisite for any and every celebration of Eucharist. Because of the circumstances of the Corinthian community, Paul had stressed the priority of community over Eucharist. Luke, like Mark and Matthew, was not faced with a similar critical community situation. These three writers felt no immediate need to enter into a theological judgment on the interrelationship of community and Eucharist. Nonetheless, Luke clearly indicates that the two are interrelated and cannot be understood except in and through the interrelationship of community and Eucharist. In 22:19 we read, "This is my body, which is given for you." The Greek word for *body* is *soma* (σωμα), which does not mean merely the human body. Rather, it means "one's entire life, the whole human being." Jesus' gift of his life has a saving meaning. "As Jesus has given up his entire life for others and symbolized that by sharing meals with them, so too must disciples give up their lives in service to others."[32] A one-sided focus on the physical body and blood of Jesus restricts the New Testament meaning of Eucharist.[33]

---

32. Karris, 716.

33. Transubstantiation focuses on the physical presence of Jesus and is therefore a limiting understanding of the mystery of the Eucharist. What is needed is a sense of action or "transactivation" to bring out the profound involvement of a Jesus community celebrating a Eucharist.

The Eucharist in the Gospel of John

The Gospel of John, as most Christians realize, is a very different kind of gospel than the three synoptic gospels. Strangely, there is no account of the Lord's Supper in John's Gospel. In this regard, Pheme Perkins lists a number of questions, most of which are difficult to answer.

- When did the supper and consequently the crucifixion of Jesus take place?
- Was the supper a Passover meal?
- Why is there no account of the institution of the Eucharist in John?
- What is the significance of the foot washing?
- Who were the participants in the supper?[34]

Since most of these questions remain disputed by Johannine scholars, it is difficult to understand the eucharistic teaching in John's Gospel if only the material in chapter 13 is considered. This is why the following passages must also be considered: 3:5; 6:51–58; 19:34; and 1 John 5:6–8. The reference in 3:5 is basically on baptism, which at the time of John's Gospel would have been associated with a Eucharist that immediately followed baptism: "Very truly, I tell you, no one can enter the kingdom of God without being born of water and Spirit."

In the Johannine writings, baptism and Eucharist are conjoined, as seen in 19:34: "at once blood and water came out [of the side of Jesus]." In John's Gospel, water was interpreted as the Spirit, which the glorified Jesus will give to his followers (7:39). The Eucharist is a celebration of the Spirit of Jesus present in a given community. The passage from 1 John 5:6–8 can also be placed in this context:

---

34. Pheme Perkins, "The Gospel According to John," *The New Jerome Biblical Commentary*, 973.

This is the one who came by water and blood, Jesus Christ, not with the water only but with the water and blood. And the Spirit is the one that testifies, for the Spirit is the truth. There are three that testify: the Spirit and the water and the blood, and these three agree.

Perhaps, it is chapter 6 of John's Gospel that indicates in fuller detail the Johannine understanding of Eucharist. Chapter 6, especially verses 51–58, deals with the bread of life. These verses read as follows:

"I am the living bread that came down from heaven. Whoever eats of this bread will live forever; and the bread that I will give for the life of the world is my flesh."

The Jews then disputed among themselves, saying, "How can this man give us his flesh to eat?" So Jesus said to them, "Very truly, I tell you, unless you eat the flesh of the Son of Man and drink his blood, you have no life in you. Those who eat my flesh and drink my blood have eternal life, and I will raise them up on the last day; for my flesh is true food and my blood is true drink. Those who eat my flesh and drink my blood abide in me, and I in them. Just as the living Father sent me, and I live because of the Father, so whoever eats me will live because of me. This is the bread that came down from heaven, not like that which your ancestors ate, and they died. But the one who eats this bread will live forever."

In chapter 13, a Passover supper is cursorily mentioned (John 13:1–3), but no description of the supper is made. In the passage above from the sixth chapter of John's Gospel, Jesus is presented as the bread of life. Eating and drinking are mentioned. Jesus is talking not to an individual, but to a group. He envisions a group which, after his death, continues to eat and drink, and this certainly took place. After the resurrection, the followers of Jesus continued to eat together in a manner that commemorated two things. First, these meals commemorated the way in which Jesus frequently ate a daily meal with his disciples. Second, these meals remembered the Last Supper that Jesus had with his followers. Joachim Jeremias notes that the earliest traces of eucharistic celebration reflect the fellowship of daily communal meals rather than the final supper of Jesus.[35]

In John, the final supper in the New Testament is connected to the Passover, which the Jewish people celebrated only once a year. However, the eucharistic data of the New Testament indicate that eucharistic meals were celebrated much more frequently than just once a year at Passover. Thus, the sharing of a meal that Jesus himself did on many occasions was the exemplar for early Eucharist rather than the once-every-year Passover celebration. Eating and drinking Jesus' flesh and blood is central to the passage in chapter 6. When we eat this bread and drink this cup we are united to the risen Jesus, who gives us his Spirit. In John, a Christian community must be enlivened by the risen Lord and by the Spirit of holiness. In other words, the eating and drinking at a eucharistic meal presupposes a Jesus-and-Spirit–filled community, and the very renewal of a eucharistic meal has as its primary goal the enrichment of this same Jesus-and-Spirit–filled community.

There is yet another important aspect of John's Gospel that Catholics need to integrate more deeply into their understanding of Eucharist. This aspect is John's emphasis on the word. Catholics generally focus on the sacrament of the bread and wine and not on the sacrament of the word. The bishops at Vatican II, however, urged that all sacramental rituals include a reading from the word of God. The post–Vatican II committees that composed the renewed sacramental rituals carefully followed

---

35. Joachim Jeremias, *The Eucharistic Words of Jesus*, 204 ff.

this instruction. In each of the renewed rituals, a reading of the word of God is to be included. In the actual practice of these renewed sacramental rituals, a reading from the word of God is seen as optional and therefore more often than not omitted. In this regard, the most egregious case of omission takes place in the renewed ritual for the sacrament of reconciliation. For the most part, when celebrating the sacrament of reconciliation, priests generally disregard the rubric for a reading of the word of God.

If, on the other hand, we Catholics would strive to deepen our love and enthusiasm for the word of God, the first part of the Eucharist, the Liturgy of the Word, would take on an importance rivaling that of the second part, the Liturgy of the Eucharist. John's Gospel honors the word, not only as *logos* in the first chapter of John's Gospel, but throughout the remainder of the gospel, the word of God plays an enormous role.[36] "Amen, amen, I say to you" is a refrain that we hear so often. The *I say* means words that are spoken, and the Father speaks in and through Jesus. Only a community that truly hears the word of God will be a community that celebrates the sacrament of bread and wine. Without the word, there is no sacrament.

Conclusions

The writings of Paul and all four gospels present the eucharistic celebration within a communal framework. The gospel writers do this in a less critical way than Paul. The gospel writers *presume* that there is a Jesus community, so this presumption appears in a more secondary way throughout their writings. The need for a Jesus community, however, is present in all four

---

36. See Michael Guinan, *The Franciscan Vision and the Gospel of John* (St. Bonaventure, NY: The Franciscan Institute, 2006), 23–25, for a very insightful understanding of the Johannine use of the term *word*.

gospels. Paul, as we have seen, is forcefully adamant: there can be no Eucharist in a community whose members do not love one another. From these New Testament passages we arrive at the following conclusions.

1. The three synoptic gospels clearly express their descriptions of Eucharist within a communal framework. They do not associate the Eucharist simply with an individual Christian's personal devotion. Eucharist and the Christian community are, in their approach, interlocked. Eucharist helps one understand a Jesus community, and the Jesus community helps one understand the Eucharist. In the presentations by Mark, Matthew, and Luke, the community is the basis for an understanding of the Eucharist.

2. In the writings of Paul, the same interrelationship of community and Eucharist is apparent. However, Paul, in contrast to the synoptic authors, clearly teaches that the building up of a gospel community is the *sine qua non* basis for eucharistic celebrations. Without a strong gospel community, any and every celebration of Eucharist becomes a diminished Eucharist. Indeed, without a gospel community, Eucharist is meaningless.

3. The section from John's Gospel, chapter 6, on the bread of life includes a strong relationship of community and Eucharist. This is apparent both in the author's discussion of the bread of *life,* which is a bread for a *community.* The communal aspect is presupposed in chapter 6 rather than ex-plicitly stated. Jesus is talking to a group, not to individuals. However, John's Gospel also highlights the word of God. The word of God and the bread of life are two basic elements in John's understanding of communal Eucharist. This emphasis on the word has been reemphasized by the documents of Vatican II. The conciliar emphasis on the word of God has found its voice in all of the post–Vatican II renewed rituals of the sacraments. In actual practice, however, Catholic lead-ers, as well as Catholics in general, have not yet developed

a parity between the Eucharist of the word of God and the Eucharist of bread and wine.

With these three conclusions based primarily on New Testament data, I have tried to establish the basic theme for this entire chapter—the formation of a vibrant Christian community is the foundation and precondition for both the actual eucharistic celebration and a meaningful eucharistic spirituality. Unless the Christian community itself is striving to be a gospel community, both the celebrations of Eucharist and the efforts at a eucharistic spirituality will be essentially deficient. The New Testament data confirm this understanding of the relationship among community, eucharistic celebration itself, and eucharistic spirituality. We now turn to a brief consideration of the early church and its development of this triadic interrelationship.

Chapter Two

Eucharist and Spirituality in the Early Church

The term *early church* has been presented repeatedly by Church leadership, Church historians, and theologians as a major formative time of the Christian community. Certain key developments in the early church have been frequently cited as determining the very meaning of Christian tradition. For many scholars, the early church includes a special group of people honorably called the *Fathers of the Church*. Together with a select group of early theologians, the Fathers of the Church have continually been cited as major formators of the Christian tradition. The foundational respect for these scholars of the early church has never been replicated in other periods of Church history, nor have later leaders of the Church merited the title of Fathers of the Church. The period in church history called *early church* remains a very special and deeply honored time.

This chapter can present only a few important issues found in this early period of Church history. These early issues are central to the three themes of this volume: the formation of a gospel-inspired Christian community, the celebration of Eucharist, and the development of a eucharistic spirituality. As mentioned in chapter 1, a gospel community is basic. How did early church Christians understand their own communities? This, of course, requires us to consider the meaning of *church*. Too often in to-day's world, the idea of *church* is heavily weighted by institution and hierarchy. Vatican II attempted to move Catholic thought and practice into a different model, namely, an understanding of *church* as the people of God. There is resistance to this, even today, by both clerical leaders and by ordinary lay Christians.

Second, there is a major need to see that the function and role of both bishop and priest are changeable. Again, there is an imbedded perception among many Catholics that what bishops and priests are and do have been exactly the same since the time of the Twelve Apostles. Such a view is not what we find in the New Testament itself, nor is it found in the early church. If we, today, can open our minds and hearts to changes in episcopal and priestly roles, then there are excellent opportunities to make the Christian community a people of God, to make the celebration of the Eucharist a celebration by the total Christ, that is, by the total community, and to develop a eucharistic spirituality that finds nourishment in and through the community itself and in and through the celebration of a communal Eucharist. Such are the goals of this chapter, and I hope that readers will see the relevancy of this historical material in the following pages.

The Beginning and Ending of the "Early Church"

The "opening date" for the early church is somewhat fluid. More often than not, New Testament writers are not placed within the framework of the early church. Rather, the New Testament writers are placed in a special period of their own. Generally, therefore, the term *early church* begins with the non–New Testament writers. Who are these non–New Testament writers? It is not always an easy task to present a list of such writers since there are questions at times of the precise dates when these early writers lived. For instance, one of earliest writings is the *Didache*, sometimes entitled in English "The Teaching of the Lord to the Gentiles through the Twelve Apostles." The Greek word *didache* simply means teaching. Some of the material in this small work presents a description of an early eucharistic liturgy,[1] but the *Didache* opens with a presentation of "Two Ways of Living": a holy way and an evil way. It seems that these chapters of the *Didache* were borrowed from another ancient source, the Qumran *Manual of Discipline*, a Jewish writing of the first century. Thus, the early church material could be dated from the middle part of the first century. However, a dating for late–first-century material is even more solidly established by a letter written by the Christian community at Rome to the Christian community in Corinth around 96 CE entitled *First Clement*.[2] Other initial writers of the early church include the letters of Ignatius of Antioch (c. 50–107), the writings of Justin (d. ca. 165), the *Shepherd of Hermas* (c. 140–150), and the *Traditio Apostolica* (CE 217). Other writers and texts might easily be added to this list, particularly the second century of Irenaeus of Lyon (c. 130–200), Polycarp of Smyrna (c. 69–155), and Clement of Alexandria (c. 150–215). We can conclude from these texts and authors that the term *early church* begins with all the writings just mentioned.

The closing date for the early church period likewise varies from scholar to scholar. For some writers, it ends with the rise of the Christian community through the efforts of Constantine, roughly around 300 CE. Other scholars, however, include the entire patristic period, which in the West ends with Gregory I (d. 604) and in the East with John of Damascus (d. 749).

For my purposes, I root the period of the early church in the Jesus communities that were established after the resurrection

---

1. There are some scholars who deny that the *Didache* in this section is treating a Eucharist liturgy. Rather, these scholars claim that the material simply describes an early Christian dinner. J.-P. Audet remains one of the major authors on the *Didache*; see *La Didachè: instruction des apôtres* (Paris: J. Gabalda, 1958). See also K. W. Noakes, "From the Apostolic Fathers to Irenaeus," *The Study of Liturgy*, 210–213.

2. A detailed analysis of the *Letter of Clement* can be found in Barbara E. Bowe, *A Church in Crisis* (Minneapolis: Fortress, 1988).

event, including the New Testament material considered in the previous chapter. In light of the theme of this book, namely, the Eucharist, I end my discussion of the early church with the Council of Chalcedon in 451 CE.

At the beginning of the early church, including the Jesus communities that began to develop after the resurrection of Jesus, the main presider of eucharistic celebrations was not limited to select individuals. Today, Catholics immediately say that only a priest or bishop can celebrate the Eucharist. However, from postresurrection times until roughly 200 CE, this was not the case. In actuality, the title of the Christian leader who presided at a Eucharist differed from place to place. In my book, *Priesthood: A History of the Ordained Ministry in the Roman Catholic Church*, I draw up a lengthy list of the titles for church leaders as found in the New Testament itself.[3] Two names in particular require clarification: *bishop* (in Greek *episkopos* [επισκοπος]) and *presbyter* or *priest* (in Greek *presbyteros* [πρεσβυτερος]). These two titles are not used frequently or consistently in the New Testament. In fact, their role and function are not totally clear. In some instances (see 1 Timothy 3:1–7; 5:17–19), the two titles seem to indicate a similarity, if not identity, of both role and function. The same can be said of the Acts of the Apostles 20:17–35 in which Paul calls the same group at one time *presbyteroi* and later *episkopoi*. In his own letters, Paul makes only one mention of *episkopos* (Philippians 1:1). He makes no mention of *presbyteros*. The writings of John speak only of *presbyteroi*. The apostles or the Twelve are never referred to as either *episkopoi* or *presbyteroi*. In the synoptic gospels, neither title is used.

Various other titles, however, are present in the New Testament, and all of them indicate leadership in a given community. In the first half of the twentieth century, Catholic

---

3. Kenan Osborne, *Priesthood: A History of the Ordained Ministry in the Roman Catholic Church* (New York: Paulist Press, 1988; reprinted by Wipf & Stock, Eugene, OR 2002), 42–44.

biblical scholars, historians, and scholars of the Fathers of the Church (called patrologists) have presented clear evidence that the threefold naming of church leadership—bishop, priest, and deacon—did not become common until the end of the third century. This dating is important. Many official documents of the Roman Catholic Church, including the documents of Vatican II and the *Catechism of the Catholic Church*, continue to speak of the apostles or the Twelve in episcopal terms. These documents specifically say that these same apostles chose their successors, who were called bishops *(episkopoi)*. In turn, these *episkopoi* or bishops called other helpers with the name of presbyters/priests.[4]

One of the early attestations of the threefold designation is in the third-century book, *Apostolic Tradition* (by Hippolytus, c. 217). It is the first document that presents an ordination of bishop, priest, and deacon.[5] This volume was written in Rome, and thus the triad of titles had become common at the beginning of the third century in the Roman area. To generalize and extend beyond the Roman area with a claim that from 217 onward these three names were the common titles for church leadership throughout the Graeco-Roman empire would be untenable.

---

4. At Vatican II, the bishops did not want to enter into this historical question, and so they simply continued the usage of *bishop* and *priest* as found in the books on ecclesiology that were written after the Council of Trent. These books presented a theology of church, in many ways aimed at maintaining that the Roman Catholic Church was the only one, holy, catholic, and apostolic Church. In other words, these books on church were apologetic in nature and written in opposition to the Protestant views of their times. Apostolic succession was one of the main arguments for the uniqueness of the Roman Catholic Church. The historical data on the terms *bishop* and *priest* mentioned above only became known in detail in the twentieth century. Thus, we have an issue today that did not challenge the writers on the Church from the sixteenth to the nineteenth centuries.

5. The *Letters* of Ignatius of Antioch and *First Letter of Clement* could also be cited as a beginning of the threefold designation. But one cannot say that in either the first or the second century, the majority of Christian communities used this threefold designation.

Therefore, it cannot be said that from the very beginning of the Jesus communities—immediately after the resurrection to 200—the person who presided at a Eucharist was always either a bishop or a priest. Other titles for the eucharistic leader are textually represented, for example, *prophet* in the *Didache* and *praeses (presider)* in Justin the Martyr.

Even in the historical material of the first five centuries, the tasks of an *episkopos* did not resemble the tasks of a bishop today. In fact, the *episkopos* during these early centuries was apparently the leader of a single-church Christian community. In other words, *episkopos* in the third, fourth, and even fifth centuries resembled today's "pastor" rather than today's "bishop."

As these early Christian communities grew, smaller satellite communities emerged in the rural areas around a particular town or city. Travel to and from the major town or city was burdensome for those who lived in these rural areas. At first, all the catechetical training and sacramental life, including Sunday Eucharist, took place only in the central church of the city. Rural Christians had to journey from their homes to the larger city if they wanted to be considered good Christians. The number of Christians in these rural areas began to multiply, and the pastoral problem of a "mission church" arose. In virtue of these mission churches, the question arose: could there not be a rural church with its own catechetical instruction and sacramental life, which would then meet the practical needs of the rural Christians themselves?

To meet this problem, an *episkopos* was at first placed in charge of these mission or satellite groups. However, his title was *chore-episkopos*, a Greek phrase meaning "an *episkopos* in the rural area." He was subject to the *episkopos* of the main town or city. Both the city *episkopos* and the rural *episkopos* resembled today's pastors more than today's bishops. Even today, we have parish churches that also serve one or several rural churches.

As time passed, however, fewer and fewer men wanted to become a *chore-episkopos* in a rural area. At that time, an *episkopos* was "married" to his Church community. Once he was appointed to a given church community, an *episkopos* remained there until his death. Perhaps the very thought of living one's entire life in a small rural area created this crisis, but scholars are not sure why the number of *chore-episkopoi* dwindled. To meet this new crisis, the city *episkopoi* then began asking *presbyters* to move to the rural church communities and take over as their main catechetical and sacramental leader. For the presbyters of that time, this move was a step upward. Previously, the presbyter, as part of the town or city Christian community, did not celebrate the Eucharist in the way that a priest does today. The *episkopos* alone was the main eucharistic celebrant. Nor did the presbyter preach. Only the *episkopos* preached. The presbyter did not administer the sacrament of reconciliation. This task, too, was reserved to the *episkopos*. In fact, the presbyter's sacramental activity was almost nil. However, when the presbyters began to assume the leadership in a rural church community, more and more sacramental tasks were gradually delegated to the presbyters. In time, presbyters began to baptize in the rural community. They were the main and only celebrants of the Eucharist. They preached the homilies. Eventually they were allowed to reconcile the sinners. This growth in pastoral ministry did not happen all at once. It took many decades for each of these different liturgical and pastoral duties to be assigned to the presbyters, and the sacramental and catechetical function of the presbyters varied from place to place.

It should also be noted that a new "ordination" was not required for presbyters to administer the sacraments. Once the presbyters were assigned to the rural Christian communities, the sacramental administration gradually became a central part of their ministry.

The growth of these rural communities changed the role and function of the presbyers in a major way, but this growth also changed the role and function of the *episkopos* in the larger towns or cities. Little by little, the centralized Christian communities developed satellite communities, and thus our current structure of a diocese slowly began to emerge. The ministry of an *episkopos* in the fourth and fifth centuries became increasingly regional. In a gradual development, regional *episkopoi* began to meet together to discuss theological and pastoral issues. In all of this, we see a slow development whereby the *episkopos* became similar to the person whom we today call *bishop*. We see this in a remarkable way in the lifetime of Augustine. In 411, the emperor, Honorius, called for a meeting in Carthage involving all the *episkopoi* of that area in North Africa. Honorius named a layman, Flavius Marcellinus, the imperial commissioner in Carthage, as coordinator.[6] The gathering was officially called a *collatio,* not a council, and the emperor mandated that the agenda should be completed within four months. Those attending included 268 Catholic *episkopoi* and 279 Donatist *episkopoi.*[7]

Considering the geographical area in North Africa (present-day Tunisia) mandated to send their episcopal leaders to this *collatio,* the total number of 547 bishops is staggering. Today, only one or the other country has that many bishops, and the territory of these countries is geometrically much larger than Tunisia. How can this small area of North Africa have had 547 *episkopoi?* Realizing that these were "pastors" of a single-church community makes the number seem more credible.[8] Moreover, since there was a Donatist schism during this same period, many cities, towns, and villages had a "Catholic" community and a

---

6. This detail is of interest, since a layperson was, by imperial command, in charge of a meeting of clerics. This instance is not the only time in early church history when a layperson was in charge of a clerical gathering.

7. Historians are not of one mind on the exact number of each of these groups. The numbers used above are indicative, however, of the large number of attendees.

8. See Osborne, "Envisioning a Theology of Ordained and Lay Ministry," in *Ordering the Baptismal Priesthood,* ed. Susan Wood (Collegeville, MN: Liturgical Press, 2003), 195–227.

"Donatist" community, vying with each other for recognition as "the true church." In the twentieth and even the twenty-first centuries, it is possible to have 500 *priests* of one or two dioceses meet together. A meeting today of 500 bishops, however, is not common for a small country. Since the *episkopoi* at the beginning of the fifth century were actually pastors of a single church, the number 547 can be interpreted as valid. In some parts of the United States today, 2 dioceses could easily have a combined number of 547 priests.

Another example of the different form for episcopacy and priesthood in the early century of the Church occurred when Augustine was still a presbyter in the Christian community of Hippo. The elderly bishop of Hippo was too ill to preach on a given Sunday. He asked the presbyter, Augustine, a well-known rhetorician, to preach. However, when Augustine ascended into the ambo or pulpit, the people hissed and booed. For them, only the *episkopos* should preach. Presbyters should not preach.[9] In this historical detail, we note that even at the end of the fourth century, presbyters were not acceptable preachers.

From the year 400 onward, the more common title for the main Christian leader of a multichurch community (a diocese) began to be bishop or *episkopos*. Only after this development can we also say that in the West the presbyter had become a lesser sacramental leader within a Christian community. Having said this, I wish to add that there were still exceptions to these particular common titles for the main leaders of a Christian community.[10]

Paul Bradshaw notes these changes. First of all, there is well-documented evidence in the early church for a change in the meaning and understanding of a Christian priest.

---

9. This small detail regarding who should and who should not preach has an echo today. The very idea of a woman preaching today riles many people, in the same way that Augustine's initial preaching riled the faithful at Hippo.

10. About a hundred years after the death of Saint Patrick (c. 390–461), the Celtic churches of Ireland called the main leaders of their church abbots and abbesses.

Although no early Christian document used the title "priest" (Greek: *hiereus*; Latin, *sacerdos*) directly to designate any Christian minister, from the beginning of the third century such language starts to emerge. This marks the inception of a major change in the relationship between the people and their ordained ministers: the latter will eventually cease to be seen as the presiders with priestly people and become instead a priesthood acting on behalf of the others.[11]

Bradshaw does not hesitate to use the words "major change" with regard to Church leadership. He further discusses a major change in the understanding of episcopal leadership.

The collegial understanding of the ordained ministry found in the letters of Ignatius of Antioch early in the second century underwent a significant shift in the third and fourth centuries. While, for Ignatius, the bishop and his presbyters constituted the corporate leadership of the local church, by the middle of the third century can be seen the beginnings of the episcopate as an absolute monarchy with the presbyters as no more than assistants to the episcopal office.[12]

Why is this history important for us today? In my view, a conclusion cannot be ignored: the role and function of both *episkopos* (bishop) and *presbyteros* (priest) has changed in serious ways over the centuries of Church life. To think that a *bishop* has always had the same role and function in Catholic Christian life cannot be maintained. Similarly, to think that a *priest* has always had the same role and function in Catholic Christian

---

11. Paul Bradshaw, "Theology and Rite AD 200–400," in *The Study of Liturgy*, 355–356.

12. Ibid., 356.

life cannot be maintained. With the extension of lay ministry after Vatican II, the roles of all Church ministries have been reconsidered. How often today do priests say, "The laypeople are now doing what we as priests used to do"? Permanent deacons today do many things that "only priests" did in the pre–Vatican II Church. Even bishops have been challenged by laypeople on the limits of their moral and teaching authority.[13]

Those early years of Christian life gradually shaped the acceptable structures of the Christian communities. In time, a generalized naming and functioning of such leaders also took place. We owe much to the early church for these forms.

A metaphor might help to understand this process. After the winter chill, a rose bush begins to push out fresh sprouts. Tiny limbs and tiny leaves begin to appear on the seemingly lifeless rose bush. Gardeners, in many horticultural books, are instructed to do some pruning so that the eventual branches and flowers of the rose will move in a certain direction. Otherwise, the rose bush, left to itself, will send out its branches and eventually its flowers in a totally unformed way. The pruning at an early stage determines the shape of the rose bush in its later stage. In this picture of a rose bush and its pruning, we see that a direction of growth is determined by what is done in the early stages after the winter chill. So, too, during the patristic or early church period, steps were taken—a first pruning—that formed the direction of Christian thought and spirituality for centuries. The next generations of Christian people found themselves in a "shaped" situation. For some, the shaped situation was taken for granted; others attempted to push the boundaries of these shaped situations. In both cases, however, the shaping was a given.

---

13. The moral authority of the bishops has been strongly challenged because of their response to the sexual-abuse crisis. The teaching authority of the bishops was strongly challenged by their insistence that birth control was immoral. These two issues, of course, are still very sensitive and divisive.

We are still shaped by what these early Christians established. For instance, we cannot address the issues of Christology without considering the early councils of the Church, which began with the first council at Nicaea in 325 and ended with the Third Council of Constantinople in 680–681. At this latter council, "doctrinal development [regarding Christology] stopped at this point. To the extent that Christological dogma was touched upon by subsequent councils of the Church, it was always simply a matter of reiterating the teaching of one of these earlier councils—Nicaea, Ephesus, and Chalcedon in particular."[14] At the Third Council of Constantinople, Christian bishops as a council made the last official statement on Christology. We, today, cannot present a Christology without taking into consideration what these early bishops did. To return to the metaphor, they snipped off the buds of early heresy and schism and thereby directed the ways in which future Christologies would be acceptable.

With this in mind, we can say that the early church and the patristic period very clearly shaped what was and what was not acceptable for Christian communities. In doing so, they also shaped what was an acceptable eucharistic celebration and what was not an acceptable eucharistic celebration. For these reasons, we need to consider the Christian community, the eucharistic celebration itself, and the issue of eucharistic spirituality not simply on the basis of the New Testament. We must also take into account the early church when the tradition of three issues was trimmed and shaped in significant ways.

---

14. Richard P. McBrien, *Catholicism* (San Francisco: HarperSanFrancisco, 1994), 480.

The Meaning of the Term Church and the Naming of Its Presider

Institutional divisions of various communities took place in the course of early Christian history. From the *First Letter of Clement* and the *Letters* of Ignatius of Antioch, we frequently hear the term *church* —in Greek *ekklesia*/εκκλησία. Both the *First Letter of Clement* and those of Ignatius generally begin with the phrase: "To the church of..."—for instance, "To the church of Corinth..." or "to the church of Smyrna...." The Greek in these letters might be translated in another way: "To the *Christian community* at Corinth" or "To the *Christian assembly* at Smyrna." These letters were addressed to a people in community, not to a single person, nor to an institution.[15] At the end of the first century and the beginning of the second century, Christians had not yet developed the institutional groups known today as "diocese" or "parish." Only gradually did these two names begin to develop in Christian communities.

At the beginning of the Christian movement, however, the followers of Jesus generally resided in or around a town or city. These followers of Jesus did meet, and their more structured meetings gave birth to a Jesus community or assembly. Thus, in the first and second centuries we find communities at both Corinth and Smyrna and in many other places. In many locales, a group of Christian men and women lived their lives and came together in a relational way. From the very beginning, Christian

---

15. Scholars have proposed several reasons why Ignatius mentions the name of the bishop. W. Bauer, *Orthodoxy and Heresy in Earliest Christianity*, eds. R. Kraft and G. Krodel (Philadelphia: Fortress, 1971), 60ff, argues that in each of these communities a split had taken place, so that each town had two Christian communities at odds with each other. By naming the leader of the community to which the letter was sent, Ignatius with his prestige is giving a signal that the community that has received this letter is to be considered the correct community.

communities were formed under the guidance of leaders. Paul, for instance, developed a Jesus community in the cities of Thessalonika, Philippi, and Corinth. A few decades later, a Johannine leader or a group of leaders formed a Johannine community of Christians. Scholars dispute where this Johannine group actually lived, although Asia Minor seems to be the more accepted locale.

One could also say that Mark, Matthew, and Luke were leaders in their respective Jesus communities. Each of the three synoptic gospels reflects its respective community's belief in Jesus as well as the author's own belief in Jesus. In other words, the three authors—Mark, Matthew, and Luke—are also witnesses and leaders in their respective communities. In their individual gospels, they presented not only their own faith stance in Jesus but also the faith stance of a given community. Each writer's respective gospel was accepted by his community as a testimony of the community's own belief in Jesus. From this common faith of a community, in many ways the Jesus community itself, in which Mark, Matthew, and Luke lived, authored the respective gospels. Mark is writing on behalf of the Markan community, and Matthew and Luke are doing the same for their own communities. In this we see that the development of Jesus communities took place through both charismatic leaders such as Paul and the evangelists. In time, other institutional leaders continued this process of community development.

The Greek term for church is *ekklesia,* which means a "calling out." For the earliest followers of Jesus, who were almost all Jewish, *ekklesia* would quite naturally be understood as a Greek translation from the Hebrew for the word *qahal. Qahal* means a calling out.[16] God called his people out of Egypt, out of the Babylonian Captivity, and out of Roman and Hellenistic

---

16. See K. L. Schmidt, ἐκκλησία in *The Theological Dictionary of the New Testament,* ed. Gerhard Kittel (Grand Rapids, MI: Wm. D. Eedrmans Publishing, 1965), vol. III, 518–36.

hegemony. In doing this, God called out a special people and made a covenant with them. God gave his "called out people" the Torah or Law of Moses. God instructed these same "called out people" to build a temple. Throughout the Bible, we hear references to God's calling his people out of or away from other peoples and other places. *Qahal* signifies God's special care for a community. Jesus also *called out disciples* so that they might become more faithful followers of the Torah and of the God of Jacob. He called out the Twelve so that they might be a special sign for his followers. Jesus did not construct church buildings nor did he establish parishes and dioceses. Rather, he gathered together a community of followers. This community, in the New Testament writings, is referred to through the use of the term *church (ekklesia)*. When we read the New Testament today, we need to read it with Jewish eyes and hear it with Jewish ears. Only then will we hear more clearly what Jesus himself said and what the first followers of Jesus truly heard. We need to hear the word, church—*ecclesia*—as a people *called out* by God to be the followers of Jesus. We cannot "hear" this word as though there were church buildings and church hierarchical institutions such as those we know today.

Note that I have not attempted to describe the various eucharistic liturgies of the early church, nor have I presented a detailed study on the eucharistic theologies of the early church Fathers and theologians. Rather, I have focused on the issue of change, particularly change in Church leadership: bishop and priest. I have done this because a very difficult eucharistic situation is present in today's Catholic Church, and our current leadership has done very little to alleviate this difficult situation. In Europe and North America, the Eucharist is available on a daily basis for almost all our Catholic communities. However, this same availability is not possible for the majority of Catholics in Mexico, Central America, and South America, nor it is possible for the majority of Catholics in Africa and Asia. Too many areas are "priest-less" and therefore "eucharistic-less." In many instances, Sunday liturgy might be possible once or twice a year. This situation is not new. Christianity has existed in Mexico, Central America, and South America for five hundred years and yet the lack of Eucharist remains an unrequited issue. In Africa, Christianity has also been present for hundreds of years, and yet Sunday Eucharist is not part of the ebb and flow of Christian life. The same can be said of the many Catholic communities throughout Asia.

The focus of this volume is threefold: a foundational Christian community, the actual celebration of the Mass, and eucharistic spirituality. How can we in the Euro-American world not grieve that so many communities in our Catholic Church are "eucharistic-less"? If we simply ignore the issue, then how genuine are our own efforts to form a vital gospel community, to celebrate Sunday and even daily Eucharist, and to deepen our eucharistic spirituality? We cannot merely perceive these three issues from our own vantage point. We need to open our minds and hearts to those Catholic communities that do not share the vitality of a true gospel community, which by its nature includes a eucharistic focus and a deep eucharistic spirituality. What and where is the current stumbling block? The answer is clear: the lack of priests. To say this, however, is too facile. One must ask, "Why is there a lack of priests today?" The answer to this question raises the issue of priority. Is celibacy the priority regarding priesthood? This would place celibacy higher in priority than the needs of the eucharistic-less communities. The Catholic Church today has allowed a married priesthood in the instances of certain Anglican and Protestant ministers who have converted to Catholicism. They are married and have families, but the Church leadership has reordained them and they serve as pastoral priests in many parishes, even though they are married and raising children.

A more difficult priority issue is the restriction of priesthood to men with the exclusion, therefore, of women as priests. Even though this issue is highly controversial today, one must theologically and pastorally raise the question of women's ordination. If even the raising of the question is set to one side, then the "masculine priority" is seen as greater than the priority of providing Eucharist for the many "priest-less" communities throughout the world.

The previous material on the early church and its evidence of change in what bishops and priests did during the early centuries indicates that pastoral need rather than ideological theology prompted the changes. The pastoral needs of rural Christian communities engendered the new position of rural bishops. This measure, however, failed, and so Church leadership in those early centuries called on presbyters to meet the pastoral needs of these early rural communities. In doing this, a major change for the presbyters thus took place. As we have seen, presbyters became the main presiders of the Eucharist, they administered baptism and reconciliation, and they preached—all ministries that previously had been done only by the bishops *(episkopoi)*. There is even evidence that at the same time (the fourth century) deacons assumed responsibility for rural Christian communities and therefore deacons as well presided at Eucharist and preached.

A major pastoral need today requires that we Catholics who enjoy the blessing of the Eucharist provide this same possibility to those fellow Catholics who find themselves in a eucharistic-less situation, and who realize that this has been the same situation for hundreds of years. Is there no remedy for this predicament?

None is available if we Catholics continue to maintain a *status quo* and continue to resist change. Three issues need to be faced courageously if the serious pastoral needs of today's globalized Catholic Church have any hope of redress.

The First Issue: There Can Be No Eucharist in a Community Whose Members Do Not Love One Another

The formation of a gospel community lies at the base of the celebration of eucharist and the development of a eucharistic spirituality. Today, however, many Catholic communities are divided much like the Corinthian community at the time of Saint Paul. Division, not unity, appears again and again. More often than not, the division focuses on what bishops and priests do or do not do. Some in the Christian community demand that bishops and priests continue to "do" all that they had "done" before Vatican II. Alongside these Catholics is another group who want bishops and priests to read the signs of the times and make adjustments that they believe are necessary. The history of the early church can indeed help to resolve this division.

The theological and pastoral role and meaning of a bishop or priest has not been uniform throughout Christian history. This insight is important today, since in the documents of Vatican II and in the *Catechism of the Catholic Church* the standard and dominant view of bishop and priest continues to be put forward as the "teaching of the Church." In this standard and dominant view, Jesus called the apostles and made them the first bishops. The apostles in turn selected their successors and made them bishops. The successor bishops called certain men to share in the work of the bishops and these men were called priests. This view became standard and dominant after the Council of Trent in the sixteenth century. This view of bishop and priest was presented repeatedly as the basis for apostolic succession. The emphasis was clearly made for apologetic purposes: the Roman Catholic Church is the *only* true Church since it has apostolic succession. The Protestant churches are not true churches since they lack a succession of bishops and priests who go back to the apostolic times themselves, that is, they go back to Jesus himself. Since the end of the nineteenth century and throughout the twentieth century, Roman Catholic scholars have tested the historical accuracy of this view of apostolic succession. This scholarly research has clearly and strongly indicated that in the histories of both "bishop" and "priest" major changes have taken place. There is no possible way to trace the role and function of bishop and priest today back to Jesus himself or even to the apostles themselves. Naturally, this has become a major issue between the top hierarchy in the Catholic Church and such scholars. For the most part, as seen in the documents of Vatican II and in the *Catechism of the Catholic Church*, the hierarchy simply ignores the findings of these Catholic scholars and continues to present the post-Tridentine approach to apostolic succession described above.

In the wake of Vatican II, the ritual of the Mass was significantly changed with the admission of local languages and with a liturgical participation by laypeople in certain parts of the Mass itself. The priest now faces the community, and many rubrics that were formerly insisted on have been set aside. All of this, in many areas of the Roman Catholic world, has created tensions within the community. In other words, the Catholic community itself is in many areas deeply divided. This division is not directly focused on apostolic succession or on the historical changes of bishop and priest. Rather, the liturgical celebration of the Mass itself has become the lightning rod for the divisive factors. We live in an age when our Catholic communities are deeply split over the manner in which the Mass is celebrated. Such a split cannot avoid repercussions on the issue of Eucharist and spirituality.

Again, I want to emphasize that a divided community means that the very foundation of the celebration of Mass and eucharistic spirituality are also divided. The contemporary area in which healing must take place in order to be most effective is the healing of the community itself. The current divisions will not be removed if Catholics simply focus on a jockeying of rubrics for the Mass. We are back to page one of this volume, where we read: *There can be no Eucharist in a community whose members do not love one another.* Church history has a freeing effect. If major changes took place at earlier periods of Church history, then major changes can take place today as well. To be open to change is part and parcel of Christian life. Liturgical rubrics are certainly not immune to historical change.

The Second Issue:
The Celebration of the Eucharist Is Based
on the Gospel Vitality of the Christian Community

When something as holy as the Mass takes on changes that until now the ordinary Catholic had not experienced, the self-identity of being Catholic is questioned. The self-identity questions both the bishop and the priest themselves. Because Catholics have been taught a standard and dominant view of apostolic succession for almost four hundred years, those Catholic men who became bishops and priests were also taught that their episcopacy and priesthood came directly from the apostles. Bishops and priests today essentially are the same as the first bishops and priests of the Catholic Christian Church. When New Testament and historical data are presented that indicate that a bishop's or a priest's duties and role today differ radically from what the apostles and their first successors did, their very identity is questioned.

Many Catholic laity are in the same situation. They want the assurance that their bishops and priests are truly the successors of the apostles. If the roles and activities of the Church leaders during and after the early church period described above are not the same as what bishops and priests do now, then is the Roman Catholic Church the only true Church? The development of ecumenical activity with Protestant and Anglican churches that has taken place during and since Vatican II only increases the anxiety of many Catholic lay men and women. It is obvious to them that change is occurring, but if change is to take place, so they argue, it can only involve secondary issues. The essential characteristics of the Roman Catholic Church must remain immutable. Among these essential characteristics are the meaning and role of bishops and priests. The immutability of the Church is challenged, if and when bishops and priests no longer are identified with the apostles and their immediate successors.

Some Catholic lay men and women are not bothered by these issues. They accept historical change as a normal way of human life. They accept the ecumenical movement as a step forward. With these alternate views, lay men and women in the Roman Catholic Church today are at odds with other Roman Catholic lay men and women, for whom an unchangeable church is almost a dogma. Once again, the Christian community is foundationally divided. Attempts to change one anothers' approach to history and ecumenism only intensify the separation. The celebration of Eucharist itself takes place in a church where Catholics will not talk to one another.

What is needed, in my view, is a serious consideration of what it means to belong to a community. There can be no Eucharist in a community whose members do not love one another. The Christian community is the foundation on which the celebration of Eucharist can be celebrated together, not vice versa. The Christian community is the foundation on which a eucharistic spirituality can be developed, not vice versa.

The Third Issue: What Do We Mean by Church?

We have seen that the Hebrew term *Qahal* is the better translation for the Greek word in the New Testament *ecclesia*. For Jesus' earliest followers, who were primarily Jewish, the very use of the term *ecclesia* would resound in their mind with a meaning different from the meaning we assign to this term today. Through the Hebrew term *Qahal*, *ecclesia* would immediately speak to them about a "called out" *community*. The first followers of Jesus, who were all Jewish (including Paul, Mark, Matthew, Luke, and John), would have such a Jewish view of *ecclesia* or church. In

their writings, *ecclesia* did not mean either a synagogue building or a religion different from Judaism. It meant *a called out
community of Jesus people.*

We today consider ourselves to be Christian, and our Christian self-identity is quite different from the self-identity of a
contemporary Jewish person or Islamic person. However, from
the time of the resurrection until the last decade or so of the
first century, the followers of Jesus did not have a self-identity
of a Christian church member. The followers of Jesus retained
their self-identity as culturally and religiously Jewish. They
attended the Temple for times of prayer. They also attended
synagogues. In other words, at the time of Jesus and during
most of the first century, the followers of Jesus, who still had a
religious self-identity as Jewish, would register the term *ekklesia*
as *qahal*, not as *church* in today's meaning. Only gradually and
sporadically—at different times, in different places, and on different occasions—did a split with the Jewish community take
place.[17] By 100 CE the split had clearly taken place, and a Christ
follower's religious self-identity began to differ from a Jewish
person's religious self-identity.

Consequently, in discussing the followers of Jesus during
the first century, I suggest that the term *church* be avoided and
the phrase *Jesus community* be used as more accurate. Also,
instead of *Christian*, I would suggest the phrase *followers of
Jesus*. This suggestion is not simply semantic. The early followers of Jesus during almost the entire first century considered
themselves Jewish. They did not see themselves as members of
a different religion. They continued to read the Torah, as we
find in Paul's own letters, and in the Acts of the Apostles, two
sources indicate early disputes over the Torah's application to
the followers of Jesus. During the first century, Paul continued
to attend the synagogues and was even allowed to speak in them.

---

17. See Frances Maloney, "Johannine Theology," *The New Jerusalem
Biblical Commentary*, 1418–1419.

Paul argued for a liberation from the Torah's commandments of circumcision and forbidden foods. In a number of instances, the followers of Jesus themselves were thrown out of the synagogue. During this first century, the spirituality of these New Testament people was by and large Jewish spirituality. Even their eucharistic celebrations were expression of their own personal Jewish spirituality.

Eventually, a lasting separation of the Jewish people and the followers of Jesus did take place; the reason for this separation is twofold, as discussed in the following paragraphs.

1. *On the part of the Jewish community,* the Jewish synagogue leaders threw the followers of Jesus out of their community. We could say, using today's language, that they excommunicated the followers of Jesus. There are several indications of these actions by Jewish leaders. The harsh statement from the Jewish community at Jamnia, written after the destruction of the Temple in 70 CE, is one of the better-known instances of the Jewish side of this separation. In the Johannine writings, which appeared late in the first century, we still find references that the Johannine followers of Jesus were expelled from the Jewish synagogues because they had preached Jesus, the Christ, that is, Jesus the Messiah.

2. *On the part of the followers of Jesus,* they also took the initiative and simply left the Jewish communities. However, as we discover in the many *Apologies,* written in the second century,[18] the followers of Jesus did not leave the Jewish fold empty-handed. The followers of Jesus claimed for themselves the Torah, since Jesus fulfilled the Torah. They claimed for the Christian community the writings of the Jewish prophets, since Jesus fulfilled the prophecies in the sacred writings. They also claimed as their own the historical

---

18. A number of the second-century *Apologies* were tracts written by Christians against the Jews.

writings (Judges, 1 and 2 Samuel, 1 and 2 Kings, and so on), since Jesus was the goal of Israelite history. On the basis of these claims as well as the Jesus event itself, we hear, in the *Apologies* of the second century, such phrases as *the new covenant, the true Israel, the fulfillment of the Torah,* and so on. The new community of Jesus, the Christian Church, had, in this view, nullified the old covenant of Judaism. The New Israel was the true Israel and supplanted the Old Israel. The followers of Jesus alone were now the true followers of Yahweh. With this self-identity, the name *Christian* became a name that separated Christian from Jew. The followers of Jesus, who at the beginning were still very Jewish, came to be a separate group and a new religion called *Christianity.*

Conclusions

Several brief conclusions can be drawn from the above facts. However, R. J. Halliburton has provided us with an important and useful caveat. He writes:

> A comparative shortage of texts, a variety of theological and liturgical emphases in different areas and in different periods, and a steadily developing theology together make the task of reconstructing a portrait of the patristic Eucharist both complex and formidable. Further, it should be remembered that the Fathers will not always yield to the questions we ask them out of our own preoccupations in eucharistic theology today, but serve us best in being allowed to express their own eucharistic faith in their own terms.[19]

---

19. R. J. Halliburton, "The Patristic Theology of the Eucharist," in *The Study of Liturgy*: 245.

Bearing this caveat in mind, the major conclusions relevant to this chapter are as follows:

1. *Community as the basis for eucharistic celebration and eucharistic spirituality.* The early church struggled to keep the Jesus community intact. The first efforts involved the struggles with the Jewish leadership itself. In time, the community separated itself from the Jewish communities in order to maintain its integrity. As it moved from a Jewish sect to a self-identified Christian community, the early church saw itself as the New Covenant, the True Israel, the Fulfillment of the Torah, the prophets, and the Jewish historical writings. In other words, the early church saw itself as a Christian Community that embodied itself as the fulfillment of Judaism. On this basis, it celebrated Eucharist and developed a eucharistic spirituality. This is seen in its use of the Jewish *berekah* as its earliest forms of the eucharistic prayer, and in its use of scriptural readings as part of its earliest eucharistic liturgy, for these readings were all from the sacred writings of the Jewish people.

   The sporadic but widespread persecutions by the Roman leadership created a need for self-identity. The early church asked itself: why are we being persecuted? The negative environment of persecution and its effects on the early church can be seen in the second-century writings called *Apologies.* These writings were defenses for the very existence of early church communities. The *Apologies* were public statements about the self-identity of early church communities. Their existence bears witness that the early church community was struggling with the issue: who are we? Or expressed in different terms: are we not an acceptable social group?

   The rise of *Docetism* in the late first century and the early second century, of *Gnosticism* in the second century, of *Marcionism* also in the second century, and of *Donatism* in the late third century were all very serious threats to the so-called Orthodox church communities. The Marcionists and the Donatists established a counterchurch group, celebrating their own eucharists and promoting their own eucharistic spiritualities, and as a result during the second and third centuries, many early church leaders were focused on the preservation of the Orthodox communities.[20] During the *Arian* crisis and throughout the entire Christological controversies of the first six centuries, Christian communities were continually faced with issues of division. In all of these struggles, the self-identity of a given community was paramount. Was a given community recognized and acknowledged as a sister community by its neighboring communities, or was it shunned and rejected by the neighboring sister communities? In the early church, the self-identity of a Christian community was a major issue, if not *the* major issue.

Today, we can take our own Christian communities for granted. In the early centuries of Christian life, the community's identity was far more precarious. The acceptance of Eucharist in a given community by its neighboring communities depended, in large part, on the acceptance of the community itself. If a given Christian community was considered suspect or even heretical, the Eucharist of the suspect community was at times not even acknowledged. In all of this, we can see again the foundational basis of community on which eucharistic celebration and eucharistic spirituality rests.

---

20. In the early church, the rise of Marcionism and Donatism caused a singular reaction. For the most part if a person was declared a heretic, the person himself was isolated. However, the Marcionites and Donatists formed an alternative church, and this is what made these two groups a major challenge to the Christian communities that we today consider Orthodox. In the ninth century, the Photian schism created for the Latin Church an alternative Church; so too in the sixteenth century the Protestants formed alternative churches. It is one thing to face an individual heretic; it is quite another to face an "alternative church."

2. *The development of the eucharistic celebration.* The scholarly study of liturgy, which developed so strongly in the twentieth century, has made us today more "at home" with historical material. Indeed, in the twentieth century, a historical appreciation of the Eucharist reached new dimensions. Today, we are the privileged heirs of this historical research. During the early church period, various Christian communities took into their worship many features of pagan worship and filled them with Christian meaning. These included the language and style of prayers, symbols such as the shepherd found in the catacombs, the kissing of sacred objects, the bridal crown, funeral meals, and dates for processions and festivals. Through the Eucharist itself and the development of eucharistic-centered devotions, early Christians transformed pagan elements of Graeco-Roman society into Christian signs and symbols. With the conversion of Constantine around 313 CE, church buildings became major centers for both Eucharist and preaching.

We need to appraise these developments as follows. It was on the foundation of Christian communities that liturgical, architectural, and artistic developments took place. Church buildings and liturgy certainly affected the growth and strength of the communities, but neither the buildings nor the liturgy would have taken place had there not been a community foundation for such growth. In these earlier times, temples and shrines were built for the gods. The Christians built churches for the community. In the early church, the Eucharist and eucharistic spirituality arose on the foundation of Christian communities, not on the foundations of buildings.

3. *The early church and eucharistic spirituality.* In the pruning and paring of various suspect communities, over a long period the early church established a foundational base that has been acknowledged as formative for later periods of Christian life. The more common name for this formative

period is the *Patristic Church*.[21] Nathan Mitchell indicates that a eucharistic spirituality not connected with the actual celebration of Mass has roots in the second century to the fifth century.[22] In some communities, some people could not attend Sunday Eucharist and provisions were made for the Eucharist to be taken to their home. Leading Christians who visited distant communities were given the Eucharist to take back to their home communities as a sign of unity. Data for this can be found from Justin the Martyr (c. 150 CE) down to Innocent I (401–417).

Similarly, in the early church there were Christians who traveled away from their home communities and who visited other distant Christian communities, even celebrating Eucharist with these communities. As a sign of unity between the visiting Christian as a representative of his or her home community and the Christian community with which he or she had celebrated Eucharist, the visitor was at times given some of the consecrated bread or wine to take back to the home community. The term for this aspect of the Eucharist was *fermentum*. The giving of the *fermentum* to a visitor indicated a communion with another Christian community in a different area of the known-world. On occasion, however, a visiting Christian was not given the *fermentum*, which was a sign that a given Christian community did not acknowledge the validity of the other community. We see in the practice of *fermentum* that community itself was the basis for an acceptance of both Eucharist and eucharistic spirituality.

Although the concern for those who were unable to attend liturgy was a legitimate pastoral issue, there was in

---

21. See John Cavadini, "Fathers of the Church," in *The HarperCollins Encyclopedia of Catholicism*, ed. Richard P. McBrien (San Francisco: HarperSanFrancisco, 1995), 520.

22. Nathan Mitchell, *Cult and Controversy: The Worship of the Eucharist Outside Mass* (New York: Pueblo Publishing Company, 1982), 10–43.

the minds of both leaders and the faithful of that period of time no intent to separate the Mass and the reception of Eucharist at home. The home Eucharist was a sign of a connection on the part of the homebound person and the community itself. In the case of the *fermentum*, a connection of community to community, and Eucharist at one place with Eucharist at a different place is also evident. A eucharistic spirituality that was not connected to the communal Eucharist and to the community itself cannot be verified in the data we have from the early church. The three issues of Christian community, the celebration of the eucharistic liturgy, and eucharistic devotion remained interconnected. The pastoral action of bringing the Eucharist into the home and the pastoral practice of the *fermentum* eventually led to a separation, but in their early origins such a separation cannot be fully identified. Nonetheless, of the three issues just mentioned, the existence and acceptance of a Christian community remained the foundation for the existence and acceptance of the eucharistic celebration itself as well as eucharistic devotion.

Chapter Three

The Scholastic-Tridentine Tradition of Eucharist

It would be shortsighted to move directly from the early church to the contemporary Catholic world. In the Western Church, two major issues bearing on the theme of this book took place. First, there was a *theological rebirth* from the twelfth century to the sixteenth century. This theology is called *scholastic theology* and the renewal of Aristotelian thought contributed strongly to its appearance. Second, both the Protestant Reformation and the Council of Trent (1545–1563) created an institutional earthquake. In many ways the Council of Trent in large measure imparted an institutionalized status to the theology of the great scholastic theologians, and therefore this chapter brings together these two issues of our Catholic tradition. From the twelfth century to the fifteenth century, the medieval Church experienced a powerful enrichment of theology, including a theology of Eucharist. The bishops at the Council of Trent used this theology and integrated it into the structures of the Church. The influence of this period of Church history lasted from the time of Trent until the late nineteenth century and into the first half of the twentieth century. This is a long period of time, and together these two issues represent a tradition in the Western Catholic Church of some eight hundred years. Such a lengthy tradition deserves mention as we consider the Christian community as the basis for the celebration of Eucharist and the development of eucharistic theology.

Naturally, given the brevity of this book, I cannot do justice to all the factors involved. I have selected three key issues from the medieval scholastic period with a bearing on our theme: (1) the theology of transubstantiation, since it focuses so strongly on the real presence; (2) the scholastic definition of *priest*, which the Council of Trent institutionalized; and (3) the medieval eucharistic devotions that in many ways contribute to an understanding and even a misunderstanding of eucharistic spirituality.

This chapter consists of two parts. The first deals with medieval scholasticism; the second part considers the institutional framework that dominated the Roman Catholic Church from the fifteenth to the twentieth century.

The Scholastic Theological Base of Eucharistic Life

The great theologians at the scholastic period continue to be well known and include the following:

Peter Lombard (c. 1100–1160), whose major work, the *Sentences*, became a textbook for subsequent generations of Catholic theologians.

Robert Grosseteste (c. 1170–1253), a major theologian at the University of Oxford and one of the few medieval scholars who could read Greek texts.

Alexander of Hales (c. 1185–1245), a leading theologian at the University of Paris who championed the use of the *Sentences* by Peter Lombard and co-edited one of the first *Summa theologiae*. In 1236–1237 he became a member of the Franciscan Order.

Albert the Great (c. 1200–1280), a German Dominican who taught at the University of Paris and at the Dominican Study House in Cologne. He did much to bring the thought of Aristotle into theology. He was the mentor and teacher of Thomas Aquinas.

Thomas Aquinas (c. 1225–1274), a major Dominican theologian whose works have influenced Catholic and non-Catholic scholars from his time down to today. His work has acquired quasi-official status in the contemporary Catholic Church.

Bonaventure of Bagnoregio (1217–1274), a major Franciscan theologian at the University of Paris. In 1257 he was elected minister general of the Franciscan Order. He and Thomas Aquinas defended the rights of the mendicant orders. He is a founding father of the Franciscan Intellectual Tradition.

John Duns Scotus (c. 1265–1308), a Franciscan theologian, was born in Scotland and became a professor at the universities of Oxford, Cambridge, and Paris. Together with Bonaventure he is one of the founding Fathers of the Franciscan Intellectual Tradition.

Many other theologians might be added to this list, but these key leaders indicate that Catholic theology experienced a major renewal during these medieval centuries. Their writings on the Eucharist provided a so-called scholastic understanding of the Eucharist. Their writings also provided a theological base on which the bishops at the Council of Trent established an institutional base for Catholic sacramental life.

Many important issues regarding the Christian community, the celebration of Mass, and eucharistic spirituality happened from the twelfth century to the sixteenth century. However, this book has its size limitations, and therefore the comments in the first part of the chapter on the scholastic period of Church history (1100–1400) are brief. I simply present an outline of the main features found regarding the following three issues: the term *transubstantiation,* the definition of *priest,* and medieval eucharistic spirituality.

The Term Transubstantiation

In today's Roman Catholic Church, the term *transubstantiation* remains a key theological term. Although contemporary Western theologians have developed alternative ways of describing the change of bread into the Body of Christ and the change of wine into the Blood of Christ, some Catholics consider transubstantiation as one of the unchangeable teachings of the Church. For them, the term *transubstantiation* summarizes the very core of eucharistic theology. The newer theological terms for the eucharistic change of bread and wine are *transignification* or *transfinalization*.

The history of the use of this term indicates that the term itself is historically contextualized. John Strynkowski writes:

> Throughout the first millennium, the faith of the Church in the presence of the body and blood of Christ [in the Eucharist] went relatively undisturbed. Diverse terminology was used to describe the change of the bread and wine into the body and blood of Christ, and theologians sought to relate this presence of the body and blood of the Lord to his historical and risen body as well as to his ecclesial body.[1]

Strynkowski and many others emphasize that for more than a thousand years, Christians believed in the Real Presence of the Eucharist without any understanding of the medieval term *transubstantiation*. A thousand-year tradition in which transubstantiation as such played no role whatever cannot be set aside as a historical quirk. Rather, the tradition of Eucharist without transubstantiation challenges a tradition that includes transubstantiation as a centralizing part. During the years between the

---

1. John Strynkowski, "Real Presence," in *The HarperCollins Encyclopedia of Catholicism*, 1080.

early church and the rise of scholasticism, theologies on the Eucharist and eucharistic spirituality focused strongly on the issue of Real Presence. The focus, however, was not on an explanation of the way in which Real Presence might be philosophically and theologically argued.

Things began to change in the ninth century. Paschasius Radbertus (c. 785–860), the abbot of the Benedictine monastery at Corbie, was the first Western theologian to write a treatise exclusively on the Eucharist.[2] In his volume, Paschasius Radbertus presented an overly realistic approach to the eucharistic change. His approach was challenged by Rabanus Maurus (780–856) and Ratramnus (d. c. 868), both of whom maintained a more spiritual understanding of the eucharistic change. Ratramnus, for his part, presented a view that Augustine had advocated centuries earlier.[3]

In the course of time, a word with Aristotelian overtones began to appear: *transubstantiation*. Guitmund of Aversa (d. c. 1095) and Lanfranc of Bec (c. 1010–1089) seem to have been the first theologians who used the term transubstantiation. In time, however, it became one of the key words for a late medieval theology of eucharistic change. All the major scholastic theologians of the thirteenth century, such as Alexander of Hales, Albert the Great, Thomas Aquinas, Bonaventure, and John Duns Scotus, used the term transubstantiation.[4]

---

2. Paschasius Radbertus, *De Corpore et Sanguine Domini* (Turnhout: Brepols, 1969).

3. In 1050, Ratramnus was condemned by the synod at Vercelli. In 1559, Ratramanus' writings were placed on the Index of Forbidden Books, since some Protestant writers appealed to Ratramnus' works. His writings were removed from the Index in 1900.

4. The first official use of the term *transubstantiation* occurs in the profession of faith required of Berengar of Tours (c. 1000–1088) by synodal action. The first papal use of the term is that of Innocent III in 1202, in a letter which he wrote to John of Belesmes. See also the documents of the IV Council of the Lateran and the II Council of Lyons, which include the use of the term *transubstantiation*.

Based on Aristotelian philosophy, scholastic theologians began to formulate their theology of the seven sacraments around a fourfold causal formula: material cause, formal cause, efficient cause, and final cause. They also used the four predicamental categories of Aristotle: substance, quantity, quality, and relationship. In this way of thinking, transubstantiation is a change in the very substance of both bread and wine. Having presented this substantial change of both bread and wine, the scholastic theologians specifically asked: what are the causes of this eucharistic change? For these theologians, there is a material cause at work in order to bring about a change in the bread and wine, since in the process of transubstantiation, the material of bread and wine no longer exists but the material of the Body and Blood of Christ now exists in its place. The material cause deals with this change of the material substance of the bread and wine that was changed into the material substance of the Body and Blood of Christ. The matter or substance of the bread and wine and the matter or substance of the consecrated bread and wine are changed, and therefore we can use the term transubstantiation. There is also formal cause at work, since the form of bread and wine is changed. The formal cause is found in the words of the priest: *"This is my body"* and *"This is my blood."* The use and meaning of the term *form* also comes from Aristotle. The scholastic theologians used the word *form* in an Aristotelian way. Matter by itself is formless. The form gives to generalized matter a distinctive and individualized reality.[5]

There is also an efficient cause. In describing the efficient cause, the Dominican theologians and the Franciscan theologians moved in quite different directions.[6] The issue that divided these

---

5. Franciscan and Dominican theologians were not in total agreement on the relationship of matter and form to individualization. Consequently, each group of theologians had its own understanding of transubstantiation.

6. The difference between the Dominican and the Franciscan approach to efficient causality in the sacraments is complex and subtle. For a brief overview, see K. Osborne, *Sacramental Theology* (New York: Paulist Press, 1988), 49–68.

two groups was based on the absolute freedom of God on the one hand and the "effective" action of a creature (the priest's words) on the other hand. The dividing issue, however, was much larger in scope than its specific application to eucharistic theology. For Thomas Aquinas, a Dominican, the very words of the priest acted as *an instrumental efficient cause*, which changed the bread and wine into the Body and Blood of Christ. The Franciscan theologians took umbrage with this human sharing in God's efficient causality. For Bonaventure, a Franciscan, the priest's words were a *moral cause* at best; the words were a prayer asking God alone to act. For John Duns Scotus, another Franciscan, the priest's words had no intrinsic effective power. Only because God had promised that when the priest so prayed, God would freely send Jesus to the eucharistic table, do the words of the priest matter. The words of the priest were totally dependent on a freely made promise of God; there was no intrinsic causality in the words of the priest. This is called *occasional causality*.

The final cause is the Real Presence of Jesus in the Eucharist. Again, the Franciscans and Dominicans had differing theologies of final causality. For the Franciscans, final causality and efficient causality in God cannot be divided. Thus, if the efficient causality differs from Dominican to Franciscan, the final cause will also differ in the respective approaches. This view has repercussions on Christology, so that the Christologies of the Franciscans and the Dominicans are also strikingly different.

All of these differences are mentioned to indicate that from the first major scholastic discussions on transubstantiation *there was no theological unity on the meaning of transubstantiation*. The fundamental dividing issue was, however, not the Eucharist. Rather, the dividing issue focused fundamentally on the theology of God. The Franciscan theologians stressed the absolute freedom and power of God. The world we live in and we ourselves are totally dependent on God. We are contingent, finite, temporal, historical, and imperfect. Everything around us is equally contingent and finite. There is nothing absolute at all, with the exception of God. Therefore, in sacramental theology God's activity is stressed. What we as human beings do is secondary. Ultimately, the sacraments do not depend on the priest, on the correct words, or on the correct matter. What *God is doing* in the sacraments is of ultimate concern. In the Eucharist, God's action is primary. Only within this context of divine action are the eucharistic actions of both priest and layperson meaningful. They are at best responses to what God is doing.

The Dominican theology stresses the *cooperation* of the divine and the human in the sacramental action. God uses in an efficient way the words of the priest. For Thomas and his followers, there was nothing about the theory of instrumental efficient causality that degraded God's position. Again, the issue ultimately reverts to a theological understanding of God, rather than a theological understanding of Eucharist itself. For both the Domincan and Franciscan theologians, Aristotelian terminology and philosophy provided the terminology for their theological presentations.

Despite the Franciscan-Dominican differences, many scholastic issues have structured the Christian community itself, its eucharistic celebration, and its eucharistic spirituality. Some of this late-medieval theology is not relevant today. However, there are major aspects of scholastic theology that have retained their vibrancy and insight. These major aspects have roots in both the Franciscan and Dominican traditions.

Walter Principe describes the teaching of Thomas on sacraments in a careful and penetrating way. He writes:

> In the *Summa Theologiae* Thomas revises his earlier view of the sacraments as primarily remedies for sin; he now sees them chiefly as specific helps for different stages of personal and social life. Thomas teaches that the sacraments are equally signs and causes, a balanced view lost by later theologians when their disputes about

sacramental causality led them to neglect the sign-value of the sacraments. Indeed, for Aquinas the sacraments cause precisely by their signifying, and they are acts of worship of God as much as causes of grace in creatures.[7]

Contemporary followers of Thomas, such as Principe, move beyond the cause-centered theology of sacraments that certain Thomistic theologians continue to maintain. With the critical editions of Thomas' own writings in the late nineteenth century, scholars are able today to understand what Thomas truly intended. The contemporary emphasis on both sign and cause and the interrelatedness of cause and sign has brought Catholic sacramental theology in the West to a deeper understanding of how symbols and signs, including religious symbols and signs, truly speak.[8]

Bonaventure, a Franciscan theologian and a contemporary of Thomas, presents sacraments in a very profound way. Sacraments, in his writings, are placed within history, and thus sacramental action is coextensive with human life. For Bonaventure, this history is incarnational history. Sacraments, therefore, are interrelated to creation itself and especially to the creation of human life. They are interrelated to the very purpose of the triune God in creation and this purpose includes from the beginning the Incarnation of the Word in the humanity of Jesus. Thus, sacraments are understood only when they are experienced in relation to both creation and incarnation. For Bonaventure and John Duns Scotus, sacraments are actions rather than things. Even more importantly, they are God's actions rather than our actions. Zachary Hayes expresses this as follows:

7. Walter Principe, "St. Thomas Aquinas," in *The HarperCollins Encyclopedia of Catholicism*, ed. Richard McBrien, 88–89.

8. For example, see Otto Semmelroth, *Die Kirche als Ursakrament* (Frankfurt am Main: Josef Knecht, 1953); Karl Rahner, *Kirche und Sakrament* (Freiburg-in-Breisgau: Herder, 1963); Eduard Schillebeeckx, *Christ the Sacrament of the Encounter with God* (New York: Sheed and Ward, 1963).

Bonaventure's theological vision can be seen as a consistent elaboration of a sacramental principle that embraces the entire world and its history. At root, this means that the whole of created reality is seen as a symbolic structure that communicates the mystery of the divine Spirit to the finite spirit of humanity through diverse levels of being and various stages of human history. Viewed from the perspective of a specifically christological metaphor, the whole can be viewed as an incarnational order. This suggest that history is a process through which God becomes ever more intimately present to created reality, not only as cause but as the object that moves and guides the finite spirit in its quest for the fullness of life. It is this mystery that comes to its most explicit expression in the structures and in the ritual activities of the church of the Christian era.[9]

For the Franciscans, transubstantiation has meaning only when it is related to God's freedom, to creation, to the incarnation itself, and to the resurrection of Jesus. When transubstantiation is focused exclusively on the Eucharist, it has limited value. When transubstantiation is interrelated to the realities mentioned above, it has enormous validity.

The scholastic period of the eleventh century to the mid-fifteenth century has profoundly affected Roman Catholic theology. This influence has extended beyond the Middle Ages. In the course of these later centuries down to the twentieth century, a number of interpretations of Thomas Aquinas took place. These are generally called *Thomistic views*. In some Thomistic views, the influence of René Descartes (1596–1650) and Immanuel Kant (1724–1804) is clearly evident, which means that these

---

9. Zachary Hayes, "Bonaventure: Mystery of the Triune God," in *The History of Franciscan Theology*, ed. K. Osborne (St. Bonaventure, NY: The Franciscan Institute, 1994), 109–110.

Thomisms are really not the exact teaching of Thomas Aquinas. It was primarily these forms of Thomistic theology that were challenged by Catholic theologians at the end of the nineteenth century and throughout the twentieth century.

A shying away from Thomism is also seen in the documents of Vatican II. The conciliar bishops preferred to use biblical language when possible and avoid a repetition of scholastic terminology. In the mid-twentieth century, several major theologians began to speak about the Church itself as a fundamental sacrament and Jesus in his human nature as the original or primordial sacrament. The documents of Vatican II echo the theme that the Church is a basic sacrament. The conciliar bishops, however, do not refer to Jesus as the primordial sacrament. Nonetheless, with the Church as a basic sacrament, the entire theology of sacraments has been rewritten. The ideas of Bonaventure on the interrelatedness of sacraments to all of history and creation and his views on the incarnational or Jesus-centered understanding of history fit well with the contemporary understanding of Jesus as a foundational sacrament and the Church itself as a basic sacrament.

The Definition of Priest

The scholastic theology of *priest* was also developed in a manner coextensive with the scholastic theology of Eucharist. Peter Lombard (c. 1100–1164) in his *Four Books on the Sentences* had already laid the foundation for the scholastic understanding of priest, namely, only a priest has the power to forgive sin in the sacrament of reconciliation and only a priest has the power to change the bread and wine into the Body and Blood of Christ in the sacrament of the Eucharist. Since the Lombard volumes became a major part of the late medieval university system, the espousal of his definition of priest was taken up by the major scholastic theologians. In this definition, the key word is *power*. Only a priest, within a Christian community, has the reconciliation and eucharistic *power*.

The effects of this definition were not realized immediately, but in the course of time, a new theology of Church became visible, namely, a cleric-lay Church. This cleric-lay form of Church was abetted by another book that became prominent in the medieval universities: *The Concordance of Discordant Canons*, compiled by the monk Johannes Gratian (d. c. 1159). In this influential volume on canon law, Gratian emphasized the cleric-lay Church. Thus, theologically and canonically an understanding of the Church as two distinct groups became in the course of time a normal reality.

On the basis of this theology of Church, the priest theologically became the major cleric, while the pope and the bishops became jurisdictionally the major clerics. The position of the priest under these circumstances has had a major effect on the Eucharist, since from this period onward the Mass was theologically and canonically under the power of a priest. Eucharistic theology therefore included a theology of priesthood. Through this eucharistic change, the presence of laypeople at the Mass became more and more a presence of onlookers, not a participatory presence. Transubstantiation became a priestly act alongside God's action. Theologians of that period began to ask a priestly question: when does the consecration happen?[10] The scholastic theology of transubstantiation grounded the scholastic theology of priesthood, and vice versa.

Of course, efforts were made to keep the laypeople part of the Mass, but with the priest alone celebrating Mass at an altar with his back to the laypeople and with the Mass in Latin (which the laypeople of that period no longer understood), the role of the laypeople became passive. The consecrated host was raised so that the laypeople could see it and pray, but again it was an "onlooking" more than a "participating" situation. For

---

10. Mitchell, *Cult and Controversy*, 151–63, provides a detailed description of the theological positions on when the consecration occurs and the relationship of consecration to concomitance and intinction.

devotional reasons, therefore, Eucharist celebrations outside Mass were more deeply effective for the spiritual growth of lay men and women. The procession on Palm Sunday in the late eleventh century had become, in certain areas, a eucharistic procession. This procession of the Blessed Sacrament even had several stations along the way at which there was a stop so that people could sing hymns and pray. The Holy Thursday–Good Friday burial of Jesus ceremony was also a procession of the Blessed Sacrament. Visiting the "Eucharistic tomb" even became a time when liturgical dramas were enacted.[11] All of this enriched eucharistic spirituality, but in a way that separated the actual celebration of the Mass from eucharistic devotions.

In these liturgical devotions, processions, and dramatic presentations, the priest did indeed play a role, but not the only role. There was much more participation not only by monks and deacons, but also by ordinary lay men and women. Moreover, the hymns that were sung, the prayers that the laypeople recited, the dramas themselves were all in languages that the people understood. Such moments were catechetical and at the same time devotional. As these devotions multiplied, the Mass itself became increasingly a priestly action. Clerics still urged the people to attend Sunday Mass, but attendance alone is not the same as participation. The Latin Mass with the priest turned away from the people continued into the twentieth century and despite many twentieth-century efforts, such as the promotion of Father Stedman's English missal,[12] the Mass remained the action of the priest with the laity as observers rather than participants.

---

11. For details, see Mitchell, *Cult and Controversy*, 129–136.
12. Joseph F. Stedman, *My Sunday Missal* (New York: Confraternity of the Precious Blood, 1938–1942).

Eucharistic Spirituality

During the late medieval period, eucharistic spirituality was fostered, but often in a paraliturgical way. In the Middle Ages the piety of the faithful was truly nourished in many ways. Lay men and women were encouraged to recite the Our Father in Latin, but if they could not do so, a vernacular form was often recited. Since the Mass was celebrated by priests, canons, and monks, and the laity were thereby confined to a back part of the church, the elevation of the consecrated bread and the consecrated wine became a major moment for lay piety. A few vernacular missals were drawn up, but since only a few people could read, they did not help the majority of the Christian faithful. More often than not, the laity attending a Mass would sing hymns at a Low Mass, and often the words had nothing at all to do with the Eucharist. After the rosary became popular, its recitation was urged by monks and priests so that the laypeople would not become overly bored by the unintelligible Latin Mass. In a later period of time, the Baroque era, marvelous orchestras would play, choirs would sing in polyphonic feasts of sound, and stained-glass windows would change as the day wore on. The people gazed and listened. They were deeply entertained, but with a special intent, namely, heaven would be similar. Going to church was a prelude to going to heaven.[13]

In the Middle Ages, the Christian community became physically, theologically, and liturgically divided: the bishops and priests celebrated the Eucharist, while lay men and women watched and wondered. In this same period, the Mass became a clerical action, with the laity in attendance. There developed a eucharistic spirituality for priests, and a basically observational or paraliturgical eucharistic spirituality for the

---

13. For this paragraph I am indebted to Clifford Howell, "From Trent to Vatican II," in The Study of Liturgy, 288–89.

lay man and woman. Such a community no longer resembled the Jesus communities of the first century and the Christian communities of the early church. Formation of one vibrant community was not part of medieval eucharistic liturgy. When the community base was changed, the Mass became the domain of clergy, and eucharistic spirituality for laypeople was in large measure paraliturgical and not centered on the celebration itself.

This first part of this chapter can be summarizing by reviewing its relationship to the major theme of this volume: without a viable and gospel Christian community, neither the celebration of Mass nor a eucharistic spirituality have any meaning whatsoever.

A Gospel Community

The theology of Eucharist, as developed in the scholastic period, focused heavily on the words and actions of the priest, as well as on the actual transformation of the bread and wine into the Body and Blood of Christ. In the eucharistic theologies of the scholastic theologians neither ecclesiology nor Christology are highlighted. The ecclesial element is subdued because no scholastic writer published a book or booklet on the theology of Church. In their various *Summae theologiae* or *Commentaries on the Four Books of Sentences,* there is no special section on a theology of Church in a way similar to the sections on the Trinity, Jesus, the sacraments, and so forth. Their studies on the Eucharist, as their studies on all the sacraments, were sacrament-focused in a very centralizing way. Christological and ecclesiological issues are peripheral.

This lack of ecclesial focus does not indicate, however, that these scholastic theologians did not envision the role of the community in their eucharistic theology. They simply did not stress the theme as emphasized in this volume: the Christian community itself is the basis for both the Mass and eucharistic spirituality. In their volumes, the role of the Christian community is more or less presupposed rather than prominently discussed.

Nonetheless, the focus on priest and transubstantiation does dominate their eucharistic investigations. Through this emphasis, a basis was established for a later separation of a theology of the Mass, which would not emphasize its relationship to the Christian community. It also contributed, as will be seen later in this volume, to the development of a eucharistic spirituality that also does not emphasize a relationship either to the Christian community or to the actual celebration of the Mass.

The Celebration of Eucharist

The intense interest on transubstantiation and the focus on the role of the priest, especially his words of consecration, centralized the scholastic theology of the Mass. On a positive note, the theological emphasis on the Real Presence of Jesus in the Eucharist provided a Christological centering on the sacrament itself. Moreover, the scholastic tendency, especially in the Dominican approach, to favor a high Christology—one that emphasizes that Jesus was truly God—also enhanced the worshipful center of the Mass. The Franciscan emphasis on the humanity of Jesus enhanced the sense of Jesus' closeness to the people during Mass.

During the scholastic period, the eucharistic liturgy became more formal and this provided the laypeople with a dramatic presentation of Eucharist. This formality and dramatic action deepened the sense of mystery. Gregorian chant added to the atmosphere of mystery, not only because Latin slowly became less common but also because the chant itself has a mysterious beauty about it. We know more historical details about eucharistic liturgies celebrated in cathedral and monastic churches than we do about the details of Mass in parish churches. The beauty, mystery, and drama of cathedral and monastic churches might easily have been nonexistent in the ordinary village church. In these churches, the Mass was celebrated in a rote manner and by a priest who spoke Latin very haltingly. The liturgy may have been eucharistic, but it may not have been very attractive.

The more negative issues that accompanied scholastic

eucharistic theology have been mentioned. First, the Mass became increasingly an action of the priest, and the lay men and women became more and more onlookers at Mass. Second, the Mass itself with its Latin, the priest's back to the people, and a barrier between the sanctuary and the nave made the celebration less intelligible to the average layperson of these centuries. In some churches, the laypeople were kept occupied by the singing of songs in the vernacular and by recitation of vernacular prayers. Neither the hymns nor the prayers had, on occasion, any relationship to the priestly celebration of Mass.

Preaching the Word of God continued during this period, but since there were no seminaries for priests, parish sermons were often simply a reading of some homily that one of the Fathers of the Church had written centuries earlier. In the theological writings of the scholastic era, word and sacrament were only tangentially interrelated. Focus on the word, for most scholastic theologians, was a focus on the words of consecration, not on the words of the homily or the scriptural readings at Mass.

In spite of all this, the scholastic theology of Eucharist with its centering on the changing of the bread and wine into the Body and Blood of Christ and with its strict connection to priestly words and actions became the foundational theology for the bishops at the Council of Trent. From the time of the Tridentine Council onward the same eucharistic theology, as we shall see, maintained its dominance. From the sixteenth century to the middle of the twentieth century, the scholastic influence regarding Eucharist and priest had a major effect on the Roman Catholic Church.

Eucharistic Spirituality

The rise of a eucharistic spirituality that was separated from the actual liturgy of the Eucharist engendered many devotional practices, some of which became extremely popular. Even the Mass itself became reinterpreted. From the Eucharist as a communal meal, the eucharistic celebration becomes more and more a ritual drama, "a solemn rehearsal of the events in Jesus' life, death and resurrection."[14] Little by little, "the communal symbols of gathering at table to eat and drink with thanksgiving have become ritual dramas of watching at Jesus' tomb while the priest pronounces sacred words which confects a sacrament."[15] The reservation of the eucharistic bread and wine increasingly assumed a significance that had tenuous connection to the Mass itself.

Lionel Mitchell emphasizes the issue of language and Eucharist. When the Mass remained a Latin-language event and the ordinary people no longer understood Latin, a major chasm arose between the majority of Christians and the few well-educated Christians (landowners and merchants, nobles and royalty, monks and clerics). This led most Christians to seek out an alternative language. He writes:

> Given the situation, it is not surprising that people began seeking an alternative language in which to express religious and political convictions....This alternative language frequently took the form of devotional speech and gesture: eating and drinking the eucharist gave way to ocular communion with the sacred host; direct participation in the prayer and song of worship was replaced by gazing at the consecrated elements.[16]

The eucharistic devotions that became more prominent during the eleventh, twelfth, and thirteenth centuries were fourfold, consisting of the following:

- Devotional visits to the reserved sacrament
- Processions in which the sacrament, concealed in a container or exposed to public view, was carried about

---

14. Mitchell, 61.
15. Ibid., 62.
16. Ibid., 119.

- Exposition of the sacrament to the gaze of the faithful
- Benediction, in which a solemn blessing with the eucharistic bread was imparted to the people, often at the conclusion of a procession or a period of exposition[17]

There is a long history to the feast of Corpus Christi. Only in 1264 was the feast approved by Urban IV for the entire Western Church. However, the celebration called Corpus Christi antedated this approval by some seventy-five years—years that included aspects of controversy as well as aspects of acceptance. The fourteenth century saw the first indications of exposition of the Blessed Sacrament for an extended period outside of Mass.[18] By the fifteenth century, the practice of such exposition had become widespread throughout the Western Church. Benediction with the Blessed Sacrament after a vernacular celebration of prayer (not Mass) developed during this same time.

The four eucharistic devotions mentioned above in some way or another all started with some connection to the Mass itself, and in time the four devotions became separated from the Mass itself. Because of this separation, a different form of eucharistic spirituality developed. In the fifteenth century, there was a clear devotional cult of the liturgy that rivaled the Mass in popularity. There was, however, no intent on the part of the faithful or the leaders of the Christian communities to pit one against the others. Indeed, the separate devotions were encouraged primarily to help Christians grow in their appreciation for the Mass itself. In practice, this result did not often take place.

From the fifteenth century until today, there are two forms of eucharistic devotion. The first form, of course, is the Mass itself. The second form involves popular eucharistic devotions, such as the reservation of the sacrament and Benediction of the Blessed Sacrament. Even today, the link between the Mass itself

---

17. Ibid., 163.
18. Ibid., 163.

and these devotions outside of Mass is not clearly understood by a number of Catholics, even by Catholic leaders.

The previous material in this chapter illustrates the major role of the scholastic period in the way the Mass was understood and the way in which eucharistic devotion outside of Mass was understood. In the Roman Catholic Church, this scholastic legacy remains influential even today.

The Council of Trent:
The Institutional Base of Eucharistic Life

It is impossible to understand the Council of Trent (1545–1563) without a fairly solid understanding of the Protestant Reformation. Therefore this part of the chapter will first study some of the key issues in the Protestant Reformation that have a direct bearing on our three themes: the gospel community, the celebration of Eucharist, and eucharistic spirituality. Second, we will consider the Council of Trent and its effects on the Roman Catholic Church, primarily how the Council of Trent provided an institutional base for the scholastic theology of Eucharist. We will also note how the Council of Trent gave rise to the issue of ecclesiology, which has major repercussions on the meaning of a gospel ecclesial community. We will also consider the forms of eucharistic spirituality that arose after Trent. From the Council of Trent until the twentieth century, eucharistic theology and the institutional form for this theology and spirituality became dominant. Only with the twentieth-century beginnings of a new reform movement that occasioned in many ways the Second Vatican Council do we find a profound reconsideration of our three foci.

The Protestant Reformation

A major event in the sixteenth century hardened Roman Catholic theology very strongly—the Protestant Reformation. Reform movements had been ongoing in the Church since 1000 CE, but no reform movement had truly resolved the problems. Jarislov Pelikan begins his volume on Luther in the following way:

> The institutions of medieval Christendom were in trouble, and everyone knew it. Intended as windows through which men might catch a glimpse of the Eternal they [the institutions] had become opaque, so that the faithful looked at them rather than through them....Captive in ecclesiastical structures that no longer served as channels of divine life and means of divine grace, the spiritual power of the Christian gospel pressed to be released. The pressure exploded in the Reformation.[19]

The late medieval Roman Curia was reluctant to reform. Many popes, even the better reform-minded popes, envisioned a reformation only if it maintained the positions of the papacy. Nonetheless, from 1000 onward reform movements had taken place again and again. The Dominicans, Servites, and Franciscans were part of these reform movements, and so were the Waldensians, the Cathari, and the Beguines. The latter three ended up outside the Western Church; the former three remained inside the Church. The Protestant Reformation cannot be seen as a sudden and unexpected event. The Protestant Reformation stands in a long line of increasing reform movements, which the highest authorities in the Roman Catholic Church were unable to handle. As Pelikan remarks, the pressure exploded in the Reformation.

---

19. Jaroslav Pelikan, *Spirit Versus Structure: Luther and the Institutions of the Church* (New York: Harper and Row, 1968), 5.

Similar to the early church disputes with the Donatists and the Marcionists and similar to the Photian Schism of the ninth century, the Protestant Reformation brought about "alternative churches." In other major crises that the Church experienced from its beginnings to the Protestant Reformation, the leader of the anti-orthodox church movement was declared a heretic. He or she may have remained active, but these heretics did not establish an alternative church. The examples just mentioned, however, in each case created a major confrontation that the Church people of their times found institutionally threatening.

Consequently, Catholic theology that emerged during and after the time of the Reformation and the Council of Trent was a theology against a differing theology and institutionality. Roman Catholic theology and institutional life itself became extremely apologetic. Only the Roman Church is the one true Church. Protestant churches were not even considered churches in the Catholic view.

Ignatius of Loyola founded the Society of Jesus in the first half of the sixteenth century. In the course of time, many well-trained men joined this Society, and as a result Jesuit theologians became a major force in the Counter-Reformation of the Catholic Church. Jesuit leaders chose Thomas Aquinas as their preferred theologian, and thus their writings on sacraments reflected his views. The Jesuits, together with other key theologians, wrote a series of theological books that were then used in seminaries to train priests (*Manuals of Theology*). These theological manuals generally were apologetic in substance and tone. These volumes presented the seminarian with a theology that, on the one hand, substantiated his Catholic faith, and, on the other hand, countermanded Protestant positions. As the number of such manuals increased, the theological authors began to offer in their presentation of sacraments additional differences and distinctions regarding the meaning of the word *transubstantiation* to the Dominican-Franciscan differences. As a result, today there is no "one theology" of transubstantiation. Even the bishops at the Council of Trent had no intention of settling the theological controversy between the Franciscans and the Dominicans on the meaning of transubstantiation. Both positions remained within the Catholic tradition.

In the Tridentine document on Eucharist, the term *transubstantiation* appears only three times—once in a title and two times in a relative clause. The very placement of the term indicates that the main issue presented by the bishops was the Real Presence of Jesus in the Eucharist, not a theological view of transubstantiation. Moreover, the opposition for the bishops was the Protestant understanding of Eucharist. Consequently, the eucharistic material must be interpreted in an apologetic way. The Roman Catholic Church has the true understanding of the real eucharistic presence of Jesus. The Protestant writers present a faulty understanding of the eucharistic real presence, and therefore the Protestants have ceased to celebrate a valid Eucharist.

From the Council of Trent onward, Catholic theologians continued to present their theology of Real Presence through one or the other theological interpretations of transubstantiation. To do this, these same theologians used the traditional four forms of Aristotelian causality. It was only in the middle of the twentieth century that major Catholic theologians began to present eucharistic theology in ways that did not correspond to the Aristotelian framework.

From the Reformation onward, Lutheran, Calvinist, and Anglican theologians developed their own theologies of real presence, which bypassed the four-cause approach of their Catholic counterparts. In the post–Vatican II era, Catholics and Protestants have entered into several dialogues on various theological themes. The Eucharist has been one of the main themes, and since the Eucharist implies priesthood, the issue of ordained ministry has also been part of these dialogues. There is, nonetheless, more agreement today on eucharistic theology between Protestant and Catholic than there is agreement on the issue of ordained ministry. This latter issue remains deeply controversial.

Likewise, in the Eastern Churches, a theology of real presence is quite different from that of the West. In the twentieth century, Western Catholic theologians became interested in the Byzantine eucharistic rite of Constantinople, which is derived from the West Syrian tradition. The Alexandrian rite of Saint Mark and the Jerusalem rite of Saint James were also studied by Western scholars, in addition to the East Syrian eucharistic liturgies and the Anaphora of Addai and Mari, who were the traditional founders of the Church of Edessa. All of this patristic and medieval material indicates that the Western theological tradition on real presence is simply one tradition among many.

The above text indicates that the Protestant Reformation presented the West with alternative churches. In time, these churches developed their own eucharistic liturgies that did not include a theology of transubstantiation. These churches over the centuries have also developed their own forms of spirituality and devotion. These forms of spirituality and devotion are centered around the word of God rather than participation in sacramental services. Indeed, the emphasis on the word of God is seen as highly Protestant, whereas the emphasis on sacrament is seen as highly Catholic. These different emphases appear in the very meaning of a Christian community (theology of church), of the celebration of Eucharist, and of spirituality.

A similar interfacing with the Orthodox Churches during the second half of the twentieth century onward has also affected an ecumenical understanding of Church, Eucharist, and spirituality. Never, in its entire history, has the Roman Catholic Church, for its part, declared the Orthodox Churches as "heretical." Rather, the Catholic Church (as well as the Orthodox Churches vis-à-vis the Roman Church) has used the term *schismatic*. Thus, Catholics can and must conclude that the bishops, priests, and deacons of the Eastern Churches are truly bishops, priests, and deacons. They must do the same for the validity of the sacraments, including the Eucharist. Since the Eastern Churches do not have a eucharistic theology centered on transubstantiation, then their specific eucharistic theologies are as valid as our Western eucharistic theology. This may sound arrogant when expressed in this manner, but it also indicates a major change in the way the Western and Eastern Churches interface with each other.

We Westerners can learn much from the Protestant experience of community, Eucharist, and spirituality, and we can also learn much from the Eastern churches' experience of community, Eucharist, and spirituality. In the three sections just considered—transubstantiation, priesthood, and Protestant Reformation—we can see that there are several ways in which a theology of church, a theology of Eucharist, and a eucharistic spirituality are developed. Our traditional, post-Reformation way of thinking is only one of many ways in which to accomplish these goals.

Let us move to the post–Council of Trent period and quickly consider again the three issues of a vital Christian community. The first section considers the period from the Council of Trent to Vatican II. Eucharistic spirituality during this period was basically a priestly eucharistic sprituality. The second section focuses on the emergence of a lay eucharistic spirituality.

From the Council of Trent to Vatican II: A Theology of Church, the Celebration of Mass, and Priestly Eucharistic Spirituality

In the pre–Vatican II Church, when the Mass was in Latin, priests celebrated the Eucharist in the sanctuary of the church, which was divided from the rest of the church by an altar rail. The sanctuary remained that special part of the church reserved for clergy. The laypeople attended Mass in the nave of the church. During the celebration of the Mass, a priest's contact or interaction with the laypeople attending Mass was almost nil. Visually, spatially, and relationally there were two communities: the priestly community and the lay community.

For all practical purposes, the priestly community celebrated the eucharistic liturgy in a language (Latin) foreign to the ordinary people. During most of the Mass, the priests had their backs turned to the laypeople, so that the people could not really see what was going on. The separation of the laypeople from the priest was intensified in larger monastic churches. In these churches, there was an additional section of the church between the altar itself and the laypeople. In this area, the monks or canons had their special places, so that the laypeople were even further detached from the priest and the altar.

The structure of a church building influenced and reflected the meaning of a eucharistic community, the eucharistic celebration itself, and eucharistic spirituality. The regulations for Mass established at the Council of Trent became the legislative standard for the Eucharist up to the Second Vatican Council. However, at the end of the nineteenth century and throughout the first part of the twentieth century, many movements eventually brought about the liturgical renewal mandated at Vatican II. With a focus on eucharistic spirituality, let us briefly consider the historical situation that led up to such a renewal.

From Trent to the Modern Liturgical Renewal

From the Council of Trent to the eve of Vatican II, Catholics generally considered the physical arrangement of a church described above as normal. Catholic life took for granted that there were two groups: the clergy of priests and bishops who celebrated the Mass and the lay men and women who attended Mass. The separation of clergy and laity was understood not only in a physical, visual, and spatial sense, but it was also proposed in a theological, liturgical, and canonical sense. In other words, the separation of the laypeople from the clergy at Eucharist became physically, visually, and spatially accepted as normal, and the same separation of clergy and laity was also accepted as normal in a theological, liturgical, and canonical interpretation. This clergy-lay type of separation was part and parcel of Roman Catholic life.

Many books were written on priestly eucharistic spirituality during the period between the Council of Trent and Vatican II. In books on spirituality, seminarians were trained to develop their own spirituality in a eucharistic way. In theological textbooks, seminarians learned that priestly spirituality was eucharistically centered. They learned that through priestly ordination a man was separated from all other Christians. Priests alone could change the bread and wine into the Body and Blood of Christ. Priests alone could forgive mortal sins, thereby enabling laypeople to receive the Eucharist. The theology of priesthood prevalent during those four hundred years centered on the eucharistic power of a priest. Ordination brought about a spiritual bond between the priest and the Eucharist, since the Eucharist, theologically, was the foundational reality that constituted his priestly identity. Some theologians even went so far as to teach that there was an *ontological* difference between an ordained priest and a layperson. The very being of the priest (hence ontological) was changed. He no longer shared the being of an ordinary Roman Catholic. He was a man set apart, physically, theologically, and spiritually. He alone among all Catholics was an *alter Christus* (another Christ).

The spiritual and theological material of this period stressed the prayerful preparation needed for the heaven-shaking celebration of the Mass by a mere priest. The same material also stressed the prayerful and meditative thanksgiving after Mass that the priest should follow in a serious way. The written material emphasized the purity needed by a priest in order to celebrate the Eucharist worthily. Priesthood was an undeserved gift that a man had received from Jesus, and the most exalted aspect of this gift from God was the power to celebrate the eucharistic mystery.

The theme of eucharistic spirituality was, for this time, most meaningfully evident in priestly spirituality. Lay spirituality was not centered so heavily on the Eucharist.[20] Lay Catholics, of course, were obligated to attend Mass every Sunday under pain of mortal sin, and obligatory attendance did in many ways center their spirituality on the Eucharist. However, for the layperson the Mass-centered spirituality was a Sunday event. From Monday to Saturday, lay spirituality was generally not eucharistically centered. Daily Mass in parish churches was at times encouraged, but attendance consisted primarily of either older, often retired Catholic men and women, or religious communities of brothers and nuns. With the development of parochial schools, mandatory Eucharist on at least one day of the week for the differing classes of children did make the young boys and girls aware of the importance of Mass beyond Sunday.

In the late nineteenth century and in the early decades of the twentieth century, the spirituality of the laypeople usually focused on the family rosary and other devotions. During World War II, more laypeople attended the Sorrowful Mother devotions than Sunday Mass. Benediction of the Blessed Sacrament was also a devotion that appealed to many lay men and women. In some churches, the Sorrowful Mother devotions concluded with Benediction of the Blessed Sacrament. After the priest had blessed the people with the monstrance and after the Divine Praises ("Blessed be God" and so on), the lights of the church were dimmed except for one spotlight on the monstrance. The people then sang in a very emotional and spiritual way, "Good Night, Sweet Jesus!" In all of this, the spirituality of the layperson was indeed touched by the Eucharist, but not in the depth and breadth that we find in priestly eucharistic spirituality. For the priest, eucharistic spirituality centered his entire day. For the layperson, eucharistic spirituality was occasional. For the priest, the Mass was central; for many laypeople, eucharistic devotion was more meaningful spiritually than the Mass itself.

---

20. See Joseph Chinnici and Angelyn Driess, eds. *Prayer and Practice in the American Catholic Community* (Maryknoll, NY: Orbis Books, 2000), xxi–xxx.

Liturgical Change

Things began to change at the end of the nineteenth century. This history of the contemporary liturgical change involves a wide spectrum. Not only was the focus on the celebration of Eucharist, but the focus was on liturgical prayer generally. This book cannot provide a detailed history of this liturgical movement, but the following list indicates the breadth and depth of liturgical change.

1833–1903: The Beginning Phase

In England the Oxford movement, led by Edward B. Pusey (1800–1882), began a renewal of the Anglican liturgy, and with John Henry Cardinal Newman (1801–1890), it also influenced the Catholic liturgical renewal. In Germany, the theological books of Johann Möhler (1796–1838) began to change Catholic thinking on the very meaning of Church. In France, the Benedictine Prosper Guéranger (1805–1875) at the Abbey of Solesmes renewed the liturgy of the Mass through a new emphasis on Gregorian chant, the style of prayer in the patristic period, a deeper union between the Prayer of the Hours and the Eucharist itself. His efforts influenced the Benedictine abbeys of Maredsous and Mont-César in Belgium and Maria Laach in Germany.

1903–1947: The Pastoral and Theological Phase

Pius X (1835–1914) became a leader in eucharistic reform with his recommendation of Gregorian chant (1903), frequent holy communion (1905), first communion at the age of reason (1910), and the relaxation of eucharistic fast for those Catholics who were sick (1911). Among the theologians of this period, Lambert Beauduin (1873–1960), a member of the Benedictine Abbey of Mont-César in Louvain, Belgium, has in many ways earned the title of "founder of the modern liturgical movement." He advocated a deeper understanding of liturgical texts and a greater participation of the laypeople in liturgical rituals. His influence extended far beyond Belgium, for his ideas were endorsed by the German Oratory at Leipzig, by the monks at Beuron and Maria Laach, and by the Canons Regular at Klosterneuburg in Austria, one of whom, Pius Parsch (1884–1954), wrote abundantly on issues that generated popular liturgical appeal. A Benedictine at Maria Laach, Odo Casel (1886–1948), wrote a monumental work on the Mass as an enduring presence of the paschal mystery. In the United States, Virgil Michel (1890–1938) was a major leader of liturgical reform, and his ideas radiated throughout the country via his *Christ-Life* textbook series. Michel in a special way emphasized the social and ethical dimension of the Mass, and in this emphasis he was a major pioneer. In all of this, the main aim was to bring the laypeople into a stronger liturgical participation.

The Reform Phase: 1939–Present
A number of liturgical reforms began to take place in the two decades prior to Vatican II. In Germany, during the rule of National Socialism, the liturgy, especially the Mass, became a special form to maintain Catholic life. This was especially true for the younger people in Germany, for whom many liturgical changes were allowed. If the aim before 1939 had been to bring the laypeople into the liturgy, the aim of the period after 1939 was to bring the liturgy to the laypeople. This means that all liturgies needed to be expressed in symbols and words that held meaning for laypeople. Pius XII (1876–1958) formed a fairly secret committee, whose goal was to reform Catholic liturgy. Many issues took place when Pius was pope: a new Latin psalter was approved; evening Masses were allowed; the general rules for eucharistic fast were radically reduced; bilingual rituals were permitted; and the liturgy of Holy Week, including the Easter Vigil, was profoundly changed. In addition to these instances of reform, the *Centre de pastorale liturgique* was established in France in 1943, and a similar center was set up at Trier, Germany, in 1947. Since 1951, an annual international liturgical conference has taken place.

From all of the above—although brief and schematic—it is clear that the bishops at Vatican II began their reform of the liturgy with an enormous amount of material already at hand. Some changes had already been made, and some changes were allowed or at least locally practiced. It would be incorrect to think that the bishops at Vatican II were the primary source for liturgical reform. The material that the committee established by Pius XII had gathered was so thorough that the very first document promulgated at Vatican II was the Constitution on the Sacred Liturgy *(Sacrosanctum Concilium)* (December 4, 1963). The bishops had had at their fingertips, when they began the council a year earlier, an abundance of liturgical material. In many ways, the conciliar bishops endorsed the liturgical reforms that were already on the table and even, in some instances, already locally in practice.

The bishops at Vatican II, however, did establish general norms for the subsequent renewal of liturgy *(SC 22–46)*. These norms covered six areas:

- General Norms (22–25)
- Norms Drawn from the Hierarchic and Communal Nature of the Liturgy (26–32)
- Norms Based on the Educative and Pastoral Nature of the Liturgy (33–36)
- Norms for Adapting the Liturgy to the Temperament and Traditions of Peoples (36–40)
- Promotion of the Liturgical Life in Diocese and Parish (41–42)
- Promotion of Pastoral Liturgical Action (43–46)

Since these norms were established by a council of the Church, they are the lens through which all subsequent renewed sacramental rites, liturgical regulations, and canon laws on liturgical matters must be interpreted. Renewed sacramental rites, newly proposed liturgical regulations, and new forms of canon law are not the lens through which the conciliar document is to be interpreted. A council of the Church has an authority surpassing later explanations of its actions.[21]

Vatican II and Its Theology of Church

Vatican II also made changes in the meaning of a Christian community. This is most clearly seen in the Dogmatic Constitution on the Church *(Lumen Gentium)*. When the bishops arrived in Rome for the initial session of the council, they were given preparatory documents containing material for their eventual ratification. These preparatory documents had been written by Roman theologians, and they were meant to help the bishops move more swiftly into their agenda. The preparatory document on the Church presented a theology of Church that had become standard, operative, and dominant since the Council of Trent. In many ways, the bishops did not find anything "new" in this particular document. It was a restatement of the dominant theology of Church for which they had been trained and in which they had lived. At first, many bishops were quite ready to endorse the material. However, a movement against the document began to take over. Some bishops from Austria, Germany, France, Belgium, and Holland had been professors at universities and were highly trained in theological matters. When they made their interventions at the council, calling for a different understanding of Church, a number of bishops began to favor a renewal of ecclesiology. The academically minded bishops were assisted in their efforts by many bishops from third-world countries. These latter bishops simply said that a continuance of the Euro-American theology of Church, which had become so standard and dominant, made little sense to the cultures of their respective peoples. Eventually, with a strong majority vote,

---

21. Even some of the regulations from the Vatican Curia do not honor the norms of Vatican II; for example, those in 37–40, which call for radical liturgical changes.

the bishops dismissed the preparatory document and created a committee to establish a new document and indicate in general some of the "new" issues that should be stressed in the new document. In itself, this was a major moment at Vatican II.

Vatican II and Its Theology of the Lunar Church

A second major moment took place when the new document, after several discussions and revisions, was itself substantially changed. In *Lumen Gentium* the opening chapter addresses "The Mystery of the Church." The light of the world *(Lumen Gentium)* was not the Church. Rather, Jesus is the Light of the World. From the very first words of this chapter, it is clear that the Church can only be understood as Jesus-centered. In this Jesus-centered foundation one experiences the mystery of the Church. In other words, in and of itself, the Church is not a mystery, nor is it the light of the world. Jesus, the Logos made flesh, provides the foundational mystery to the Church and provides any and all light that the Church claims. Some of the bishops at Vatican II used a patristic metaphor. Jesus, like the sun, is the Light of the World. The Church is similar to the moon. The moon of itself has no light of its own. The moon reflects the light of the sun. So, too, the Church is Church only when the Church reflects Jesus. When the Church does not reflect Jesus, it resembles a corporate institution, similar to IBM and Intel.

Vatican II and Its Theology of the People of God

A third change of a theology of Church occurred when the second chapter of *Lumen Gentium* was on the agenda for discussion. The second chapter is entitled "On the People of God." However, a strong minority group of bishops wanted the theme of the second chapter to be "The Hierarchy of the Church." In other words, the text would move from the foundational mystery of the Church to the pope and bishops. Arguments pro and con took up no small amount of time, but in the end the bishops by a wide majority opted for "On the People of God." The text moves from the mystery of the Church to every Christian man and woman, for these through baptism and confirmation constitute the people of God.[22]

The Christian community, as I have stressed many times, is the foundation for the eucharistic celebration and for eucharistic spirituality. In the twenty-first century, the Christian community primarily means the Church as lunar mystery and the Church as the people of God. The hierarchical dimension of the Christian community, though extremely important, is not the constitutive foundation in Vatican II ecclesiology. Indeed, the hierarchical nature of the Church, which is chapter 3 in *Lumen Gentium*, makes sense only on the basis of the lunar Church reflecting Jesus and the constitution of all the baptized/confirmed (and this includes popes and bishops) as the people of God. In other words, chapter 2 of *Lumen Gentium* speaks of a people of God who are constituted by the Lord himself and who at this foundational level are all of equal status.

It is evident that major changes regarding ecclesiology took place at Vatican II. The three issues mentioned above—Jesus alone is the Light of the World, the Church is lunar, and the people of God constitute the basis for any further hierarchical structure—indicate the major renewal in ecclesiology that the council expressed in a very clear way. Other changes regarding Church were also made, but these other changes are secondary to these three.

A Postconciliar Church

Today, we live in a post–Vatican II Church, and a postconciliar time has been and is today a very distinct time of Catholic life. After every major council in the past, there has been a lengthy

---

22. My preference would have been to include Eucharist with baptism and confirmation, since the sacrament of initiation is truly baptism-confirmation-Eucharist. The bishops at Vatican II make no mention of Eucharist as part of the sacramental initiation into the people of God.

period of unrest and distrust. This is seen in the aftermath of the very first council of the Church, the Council of Nicaea in 325. The same is true for the second council, the Council of Constantinople (381), and for other early councils: the Council of Ephesus (431) and the Council of Chalcedon (451). Major councils in later centuries also experienced a tense time in their aftermath: the Fourth Council of the Lateran (1215), the Council of Constance (1414–1418), the Council of Trent (1545–1563), and the First Vatican Council (1869–1870). Vatican II is no different. We live in an atmosphere of division, hesitation, and even confusion. We also live in an atmosphere of renewal, rebirth, and expectation. A postconciliar church is a church of mixed emotions and feeling, of hesitation and exaltation, and of unclarity and yet clarity.

Dioceses and parishes today continue to have this kind of postconciliar atmosphere. Differing scholars and Church leaders are not in accord with the exact meaning of particular conciliar texts, and so there are arguments pro and con over several major issues. There are some Catholics who have simply disregarded the prescriptions of Vatican II, while others find issues in the conciliar documents that they like and so they run nine yards with their interpretation. Some Catholics have even left the Church—one group even established an alternative church—or have ceased to attend Church services. We probably have two more generations of Catholics before the major divisive issues reach some sort of rapprochement.

Repeatedly, the lightning rod for this divisiveness has been the liturgy, but even more precisely stated, the eucharistic celebration itself. Issues about the Mass have divided a diocese and a parish. Even some families have experienced tension on eucharistic matters. The issues might be kneeling or not kneeling, giving the kiss of peace or not giving the kiss of peace, the presence of women in the sanctuary or the absence of women in the sanctuary, and the list could go on. Actually, in most cases, the particular issue that flares up is not the most important item.

Generally, there is something far more profound than kneeling or not kneeling, and so on, at the heart of the matter.

I have no suggestions on how to bring a postconciliar church to unity, nor does the pope or the bishops. Since a time of distress has followed all major councils of the past, we today need to consider this period of stress as a normal reaction to a council. Having disclaimed any magic medicine for this situation, I want to add that a postconciliar division in a diocese, a parish, or a religious community is not something to be tolerated with a *laissez-faire* approach. A Christian community needs to take seriously a statement that has been used several times in this book: *There can be no Eucharist in a community whose members do not love one another.* If there is no gospel community, eucharistic celebrations will falter and eucharistic spirituality will dry up. The key approaches that need to enter into the postconciliar situation include the following:

- Respect for one another even if there are differences in one's stance
- A return again and again to the gospels for guidance when divisions begin to appear
- Harmony rather than either-or as the goal
- The Church is a Church of sinners, not a Church of only saints
- Love the sinner, and at the same time admit that you, too, are a sinner

This book not only has stressed the Christian community but also the interconnection of community, Mass, and eucharistic spirituality, which has appeared many times. All three issues were affected by the Council of Trent, some four hundred plus years ago, and by the Second Vatican Council only forty years ago. We could express this interconnection to theology, Mass, and spirituality as follows.

- The modern liturgical movement has in major ways transformed the *theological understanding* of both the Christian community and the Eucharist, which had become standard from the Council of Trent to the middle of the twentieth century.

- The modern liturgical movement has in a major way transformed the *pastoral understanding* of the Christian church and the Eucharist, which had become standard from the Council of Trent to the middle of the twentieth century.

- The modern liturgical movement has in a major way transformed the *eucharistic spirituality*, which had become standard from the Council of Trent to the middle of the twentieth century.

All three of these issues have changed in a major way during this same period because the standard theology of Church, which had officially dominated the Catholic Church from the Council of Trent to the late twentieth century, has been called into question and new theologies of the Church have been formulated. As of today, a new theology of Church has not been totally established, but a change in ecclesiology has been and is continuing to take place. Today, we are in the middle of this ecclesiological change. If the theological understanding of the Christian community, that is, the standard and dominant ecclesiology itself, is undergoing radical change, then we cannot help but experience change in the way that the Eucharist is celebrated and change in the way that a eucharistic spirituality becomes vibrant. We are back at the thesis of this volume: it is the gospel community of Christians that is the bedrock or foundation of eucharistic celebration and eucharistic spirituality. The bedrock is slowly being reformulated, and this, therefore, has repercussions on the celebration of the Mass and the living out of a eucharistic spirituality.

Before any conclusions can be drawn on the material presented so far in this chapter, we move to a theme that hopefully will complete the major details needed for any conclusions on this delicate matter of renewal. The emphasis in the previous material has been on priestly eucharistic spirituality, which received the lion's share of attention from the Council of Trent to Vatican II. Lay spirituality did not receive much attention from Church authorities during this same time. In order to have a complete understanding of eucharistic spirituality, we need to move beyond priestly eucharistic spirituality and focus as well on lay eucharistic spirituality.

From the Council of Trent to Vatican II : Lay Eucharistic Spirituality

From the Council of Trent to the Second Vatican Council, the ordinary lay woman and man in the Western Roman Catholic Church attended Mass, and thus the Eucharist was indeed a major part of their spirituality. In contrast to the priestly eucharistic spirituality, the lay eucharistic spirituality during this period of Western Roman Catholic history took on a different form.

Eucharistic Spirituality
Eucharistic Celebration
An Ideally Gospel-Inspired Community of Faith

The Ideal Community of Faith

Perhaps it is best to begin with the ideal community of faith. Naturally, such an ideal community of faith has never existed. Nonetheless, the ideal has enlivened many efforts for the building of community, which one finds in our Church history. The diagram helps us grasp the ideal interconnection of spirituality-Eucharist-community, and this ideal formulation is precisely what Paul had in mind in his First Letter to the Corinthians.

In the diagram on the previous page, the gospel-inspired community of faith is the foundation for the celebration of Mass and the development of eucharistic spirituality. The gospel-inspired community is an ideal, since each Christian community is a genuine Christian community only if its members are striving for gospel ideals. If the foundation of a Christian community begins to erode due to divisions over liturgical issues, gender issues, hierarchical issues, and tradition-inspired issues, then the entire superstructure will also give way. Given a foundational weakness, it would be foolish to concentrate on eucharistic spirituality or even on the celebration of Mass to remedy the foundational weaknesses. The foundational weakness must be faced; otherwise, the community is being built on sand. In this current period of postconciliar Church, divisions and anger are "normal." Our current Church life does not differ from any preceding postconciliar Church life. In looking back and studying these other postconciliar periods, perhaps we will find help for coping with our own present situation.

In addition to reflecting on these former postconciliar times, we should also reflect on the Corinthian community at the time of Paul. Paul encountered division and distrust in the existential celebration of Eucharist by the Corinthian community. However, despite his stern criticism of its actual celebration of the Lord's supper, he was pointedly more anxious and angered about the gospel quality of their community itself. In his view, only a renewal of the gospel community itself would enable the

Corinthians to overcome their eucharistic blemishes. This is a powerful model for today's postconciliar Church communities where eucharistic dissension exists.

In today's world, the community remains central for the eucharistic celebration. However, a contemporary understanding of community is different from that found in the New Testament writings. In contemporary society, *community* is an elusive term, since it can refer to many examples of human life. Perhaps the family remains the primary exemplar for community, but as we know so well, the communal activity of family life is often secondary to economic concerns, such as work hours, single-parent families, and so on. Nonetheless, family communal life still energizes our contemporary society.

A second area with a major role in daily life includes non-family structures. Men and women need friends, and a circle of friends—therefore a *community*—is a highly valued desideratum for many people. The need to share aspects of one's life with friends rather than with family is a needed part of today's world.

Another nonfamily community that in some instances is very important is economic. One's business or career position often needs the acceptance and honor of the business community. In other words, an individual may have a job, but if others do not respect the person in such a job, the person is isolated and the work is drudgery. However, when the person's work is respected by others, this community of others makes the person's workday worthwhile. Business executives, for instance, need the respect of others if they wish to remain in office.

Other examples of communities could also be mentioned. In schools, younger people form a community of friends. Older people who are alone form a community of friends. Cultural groups form a community of cultural groups. In all of these examples, certain cautionary characteristics regarding community appear:

- *Communities are not either-or, but more-or-less.* Even in family circles, there are stages during which the family community is more tightly bound to one another and stages when family bonds are stretched to the breaking point. Church communities are similar. The fact that there are a large number of people gathered inside a church building does not of itself indicate that all of the people are at the same stage of communal relationship. Church communities must take the time and make the effort to bring about a Christian interrelationship with one another. In Catholic megachurches today, many people are basically onlookers and not really participants. In these megaparishes, usually a small group of people "runs the show." Other Catholic churches today face cultural tensions, which disaffect the formation of a Christian community, and only in time can such cultural differences be resolved. At times, however, no cultural interrelationship takes place, and one cultural group is socially and *de facto* excommunicated from the basic church group.

- *Communities come and go.* Many parishes have indeed, through major efforts, formed a vibrant community. More often than not, the catalyst that created such vibrant communities has been the liturgy. Catholics flock to a given church because either the liturgy or the homily is superior and more deeply spiritual than they find in other churches. In some dioceses, a given bishop is a vibrant pastoral leader and is able to affect the majority of the Catholics in the diocese in a very spiritual and gospel manner. When this bishop is replaced, the successor could be a person of a very different ilk. He could be autocratic or overly Rome-oriented or even disinterested in the basic pastoral needs of the diocese. Pastors are similar. One pastor can be seen as a God-sent gift to the community, and his successor is seen as a tyrant.

- *Communities are too large.* In some Protestant churches, whenever the pastor cannot recognize the growing number of members in the community, it is a signal for the church to divide. In the Catholic Church today, such a signal means little, since any division of a parish means the presence of more priests, and we suffer from a dearth of priests. This lack of priests is especially noticeable in Mexico, Central America, and South America. It is also present among the native peoples of North America. Many rural areas of the Philippines share the same problem: no priests for many people. Roman Catholic missionaries have, since the sixteenth century, baptized men and women in all of these areas, and in the past four hundred or so years they have left baptized communities with no eucharistic celebrations. In some place, a eucharistic celebration is possible once or twice a year, but not more often. Such a situation is theologically and juridically reprehensive, and Church leadership over the centuries has so far done little to alleviate this eucharistic deprivation. Remarkably, the people who are thus baptized but have no Sunday Eucharist have creatively developed a spirituality. It is not, however, a eucharistic spirituality.[23]

A major question immediately arises: what kind of Christian community is needed to ground both the celebration of Eucharist and the development of a eucharistic spirituality? Throughout the many centuries of Church history, this question has engendered many answers, and even today the issue of this triadic relationship is presented theologically in a variety of ways.

---

23. This kind of noneucharistic spirituality is found among the Native Americans, such as the Acoma, Pueblo, Zuni, Navajo, and O'Oton. In these communities, the spirituality is focused on tribal celebrations that in some ways might contain a Christian ingredient, but for the most part, the rituals reflect the Native American culture itself.

Institutionally Established Christian Communities

Before focusing directly on the several major answers to the question of this relationship, a factual situation should be noted. Attendance at Sunday Mass has decreased considerably in today's Roman Catholic parishes throughout the United States. Pastors and parish staffs, therefore, have focused on remedial measures. Their primary remedial measure, in most cases, focuses on the quality of the eucharistic liturgy itself. In order to encourage parishioners to attend Mass, pastors and the parish staffs have generally centered their energies on improving the Sunday eucharistic liturgy. The choir is upgraded to a semiprofessional status. The décor of the altar area is enhanced by floral arrangements and artistic banners. A ministry of greeters is established to welcome people as they enter the church. Church bulletins are vastly improved through a professional-looking layout. Diligent efforts are made to improve Sunday homilies. Pastors and parish councils have exerted a great deal of energy to make the Sunday eucharistic liturgy a prayerful service that hopefully will draw more and more people to Sunday Mass. Surely, all of us—in one way or another—have experienced a parish in which such major efforts were made to enhance Sunday liturgy. This exertion of energy, expenditures of money and time, and the detailed planning of each Sunday's eucharistic celebration have had a single purpose: to improve the celebration of the eucharistic celebration so that more people will attend Sunday Mass.

Over the course of time, some of these parishes have run out of energy, and the Sunday liturgy begins to assume a more mundane and formalized character. People notice this, and as a result the number of people at the Sunday celebration of the Mass begins once again to dwindle. A major question arises for all of this effort: what went wrong? The immediate answer is that the Sunday eucharistic liturgy has become humdrum and needs to be re-enlivened once again. Pastors and parish councils have continually focused on liturgy as the central drawing point for the local church. Their intention is good, but the choice of liturgy as the starting point is the Achilles' heel, which has helped but has not resolved the primary issues.

The notion that a community of faith, eucharistic celebration, and eucharistic spirituality are intertwined is not a new way of thinking. The *Catechism of the Catholic Church* echoes Murphy-O'Connor's emphasis on "Christ" as the celebrant of a sacrament. In paragraph 1136 the text of the *Catechism* answers the question posed in the very title of this part of the *Catechism*, namely: "Who celebrates?" The answer is stated succinctly: "Liturgy is an 'action' of the *whole Christ (Christus totus)*" [italics and Latin are in the original text]. This same idea is repeated in paragraph 1140: "It is the whole *community*, the Body of Christ united with its Head, that celebrates" [italics are in the original text]. A community, *totus Christus*, celebrates the Church's eucharistic liturgy. The eucharistic liturgy is not celebrated simply by the priest. The Church is a community of faith, and consequently the eucharistic action is a community celebration dependent on the very existence of a Christian community. Only on the basis of this fundamental Christian community and its subsequent celebration of the eucharistic meal is there a possibility for a eucharistic spirituality. This triadic relationship of spirituality, eucharistic celebration, and a community of faith constitutes the heart of this present book.

The community of faith, however, can be defined in many ways, and throughout Church history the community of faith has appeared in many forms. Not all eucharistic devotions and forms of spiritual during this lengthy period can be considered the best way to celebrate the Eucharist. Saint Paul would have had a great deal to say negatively about benediction, private visits to the Blessed Sacrament, and Corpus Christi processions. The focus of his critique would be that the center of such spirituality is devotion, not the actual eucharistic celebration that we call the Mass. This can be seen in three distinct forms.

1. In many instances, even today, the chapel in which the Blessed Sacrament is reserved is far more elaborately decorated than the altar itself. There are many more flowers on the ledge in front of the tabernacle than on the main altar of the church. There are more candles burning in front of the tabernacle than on the altar in the church itself. In other words, the visual décor for the tabernacle upstages the visual décor of the main altar in the church. To rephrase the famous remark of Queen Victoria, Saint Paul would not be amused.

2. On Holy Thursday there is the procession to the so-called altar of repose. This takes place today on Good Friday itself. However, in many churches and chapels the altar of repose is decorated in an elegant manner, and people come to spend an hour or so at the altar of repose. Once again, the décor of the altar of repose surpasses the décor of any celebration of the Eucharist in the main part of the church with perhaps the exception of Christmas. Saint Paul would not be amused.

3. On the feast of Corpus Christi, there are elaborate processions, with benediction given in three different places, all of which have altars richly decorated with flowers, banners, pictures, and incense. Again, Saint Paul would not be amused.

The forms of lay eucharistic spirituality during the centuries from Trent to Vatican II were indeed eucharistic spiritualities, but they were largely *devotional* spiritualities: they focused on private devotion more than on the actual celebration of the Lord's supper. The community of faith was present in the many lay men and women, and their faith was genuine. However, their faith was more personal than communal; more prayer-centered—that is, on *devotional* prayers—than eucharist-centered; and more nonsacramental than sacramental. Such a eucharistic spirituality, despite all its good points, does not truly measure up to the ideal eucharistic spirituality described previously in which the three entities form an integrated whole.

Efforts today to combine both priestly and lay eucharistic spiritualities into a meaningful unity are clearly evident. The deficiencies of both the priestly and lay eucharistic spiritualities are clear, and the efforts to combine the two are rightly praised.

Conclusions

This has been a lengthy chapter, covering an enormous amount of material. Naturally, the minute details of this material could not be considered, nor could all the causes, historical circumstances, and theological reasons for the many themes presented be given. I have used a "broad brush" to gather these ideas. What honest conclusions can be made from such a broad-brush description? I offer the following.

1. Scholastic theology needs to be perceived as a time of major theological renewal in the Western Church. Its positive features cannot be minimized. Even today, we continue to rely on many issues presented by the late medieval theologians. Nonetheless, like everything created, scholastic theology has its limits. The Western world, since the medieval times, has undergone major changes. First was the period of enlightenment, modernization, and scientific discovery. Second, an ongoing contemporary period called postmodernization is transforming the Western world in a manner that can only be described as a paradigmatic shift of thinking. The medieval mindset, both philosophically and theologically, no longer speaks to the postmodern individual. Can we today, then, find a theological form of communication that speaks to the modern Western person? If not, then we may think we are spreading the good news, but no one is able to hear the good news. Evangelization is

indeed a proclamation of the good news, but one needs ears to hear it. This interplay of speaker and hearer is a major issue today, and as such it raises the question whether the language and thought patterns of scholastic theology are meaningful. Or, are these patterns a foreign language and therefore unintelligible?

2. A second conclusion, only hinted at occasionally in this chapter, is the globalization of today's world and therefore of today's Christian world as well. Globalization involves the intersection of cultures. For some people, globalization is simply a new form of colonization, since globalization favors the developed world over the developing world. The cultures of the developed world are on one side, and the cultures of the developing worlds are on the other side, and the balance is uneven.

Scholastic theology and Tridentine institutionality are Western and therefore cultural to the core. The gospel, as it has been translated by scholastic theology and Tridentine theology, is also cultural to the core. Thus, the question arises: can we Christians translate the gospel message into other cultural forms, or can the gospel only be preached in its current Euro-American form? To answer these questions would require a lengthy volume in itself. However, part of the postconciliar atmosphere of today's Church involves the issue of many cultures. In Asia, the term *globalization* is not appreciated, and so Asians have begun to develop a different term: *glocalization*, a combination of global and local. Currently there is a major struggle between the Vatican Curia and many local theologians and clergy in such areas as Asia and Africa. The Vatican Curia stresses the global, and the theologians and clergy stress the local. The intersection of cultures is simply a current fact of Christian life, and the cultural issue affects the very meaning of a local Christian community, a local celebration of Eucharist, and a local development of eucharistic spirituality. Many authors today use the term *multicultural*. My preference is to use the term *equicultural*, since this latter term does not suggest that one culture is the benchmark for all the others. It is also a term that respects the God-given dignity of every human being, regardless of individual cultures.

3. This chapter has clearly noted that a theological understanding of the Church has been changed by the bishops at Vatican II. The Tridentine and post-Tridentine ecclesiology can no longer be considered the dominant theology of Church. Vatican II ecclesiology is centered on Jesus, the Light of the World; the Church itself is lunar, which means it has no light of its own and is truly Church only when it reflects Jesus, the Light of the World. The basic understanding of Church is not clergy-laity, but people of God. Only in the light of this ecclesiology can we today develop gospel communities, celebrate Eucharist, and develop eucharistic spirituality.

Two other items are needed to complete this view of Church, and these are considered in the final chapter.

Chapter Four

The Eucharistic Community, Celebration, and Spirituality: Contemporary Challenge

Two theological issues were stressed in the documents of Vatican II. On the one hand, both issues moved beyond the scholastic-Tridentine tradition, and on the other hand, both issues can be found in the New Testament and in the early Fathers of the Church. The documents of Vatican II, therefore, offer something new and at the same time something old. It is new since for eight hundred years the scholastic-Tridentine tradition did not stress these two issues. It is something old since the writers of the New Testament and the early Church Fathers did stress both issues.

Today's Catholics are challenged by these two issues. The first issue is to widen our thinking on Eucharist. Eucharist is twofold: *the Eucharist of the word* and the *Eucharist of the bread and wine*. The second issue is even more expansive, for here we are challenged to see the relationship between *the Eucharist of the Lord's table* and *the Eucharist of the world itself*. Each of these is considered in detail in the following sections.

The Eucharist of the Word
and Eucharist of the Bread and Wine

The Eucharist, that is, the celebration at Mass, involves readings from the sacred Scriptures (the word of God) and the celebration of the eucharistic meal. This word-meal celebration is, in the documents of Vatican II, referred to as the apex of the Church's life. In the Constitution on the Sacred Liturgy *(Sacrosanctum Concilium)*,[1] we read:

> ...the liturgy is the summit toward which the activity of the Church is directed; it is also the fount from which all her power flows (10).

> The treasures of the Bible are to be opened up more lavishly [in the celebration of Eucharist] so that a richer fare may be provided for the faithful at the table of God's word. In this way the more representative part of the sacred scriptures will be read to the people in the course of a prescribed number of years (51).

> Sacred scripture is of the greatest importance in the celebration of the liturgy (24).

> In sacred celebrations a more ample, more varied, and more suitable reading from sacred scripture should be restored (35).

The reading of the word of God, which was in the past called "Mass of the Catechumens," is officially today seen as integral to eucharistic service. In *Sacrosanctum Concilium,* we read:

---

1. Conciliar documents are abbreviated after first mentioned as follows: *Sacrosanctum Concilium, SC; Lumen Gentium, LG.*

The two parts which in a sense go to make up the Mass, viz. the liturgy of the word and the eucharistic liturgy, are so closely connected with each other that they form but one single act of worship. Accordingly this sacred Synod strongly urges pastors of souls that, when instructing the faithful, they insistently teach them to take part in the entire Mass, especially on Sundays and holy days of obligation (56).

In the same conciliar document (*SC* 41), we hear that the celebration of the Eucharist is the principal manifestation of the Church. In the Dogmatic Constitution on the Church *(Lumen Gentium,* 26) we are told that the bishops, above all in the Eucharist that they themselves offer, manifest the fullness of the Church. In these passages, the Eucharist includes the real presence of Jesus in both the Word of God and in the sacramental bread and wine. Together, such a Eucharist is the principal manifestation of the fullness of the Church. Together, as we read in the conciliar citations above, the two form but one single act of worship.

Carol M. Norén, when she was a professor of homiletics at the Divinity School in Duke University, has gathered together both the Protestant and Catholic material on "The Word of God in Worship: Preaching in Relationship to Liturgy."[2] In this essay, she draws together the major statements and directives of Protestant and Roman Catholic leadership since Vatican II. Both of these leaderships attempts have enriched eucharistic thought by their interventions. She writes:

> Protestants are anxious to show that preaching is a legitimate enterprise to be placed alongside, but not to replace, the sacred ministry of the Church, while Roman

---

2. Carol M. Norén, "The Word of God in Worship: Preaching in Relationship to Liturgy," in *The Study of Liturgy,* 31–51.

Catholics are equally determined to demonstrate the sacramental nature of preaching itself and to restore it to respectability in the Catholic tradition.[3]

In the course of her essay, she cites a Catholic theological scholar, Eduard Schillebeeckx, who writes:

At its peak, the word itself becomes sacrament....Because the sacrament is entirely fruitful only in the one who receives by faith the gift which Christ makes of himself in the sacrament the ministry of the Word (whose internal effect is the obedience in faith to the salvation brought to us by God in Christ) is necessarily directed toward the ministry of the Sacrament. What is begun in the word is perfected in the sacrament.[4]

Schillebeeckx skillfully brings together the insights of the bishops at Vatican II, who, as we have seen above, stressed the relationship of word and Eucharist. This relationship is mutual, and therefore the sacramentality of the consecrated bread and wine permeates the sacramentality of the liturgical word of God. In Schillebeeckx's view, sacramentality cannot be predicated of one without predicating it as well of the other.

Norén selects a passage from Jean-Jacques von Allmen as indicative of the current Protestant effort to unite the table of the word and the table of the bread and wine. Von Allmen writes:

Divine worship is an eschatological event. Its whole procedure is a sort of echo of the incarnation and prefiguration of worship in heaven. It is an echo of the incarnation in that it includes, like the ministry of Jesus,

---

3. Ibid., 35. Norén bases her statement on D. E. Babin, "Toward a Theology of Liturgical Preaching," *Anglican Theological Review* 52 (1970): 228.

4. Eduard H. Schillebeeckx, "Word and Sacrament and the Church," *Listening* (Winter 1969), 32.

what one could call a "Galilean" moment—centred on the sermon—and a "Jerusalemite" moment—centred on the Eucharist.[5]

Prior to Vatican II, the official Church had prescribed Sunday attendance at Mass in such a way that if one were not present for the eucharistic prayer and communion, one committed a mortal sin. On the other hand, if one were late and came to Mass, missing only the "Mass of the catechumens," the moral guilt was "only a venial sin." This mortal-venial distinction hardly fits with the Vatican II understanding that "the liturgy of the word and the eucharistic liturgy, are so closely connected with each other that they form but one single act of worship" (SC 56). This is not to say that coming late to today's eucharistic celebration is a mortal sin, but it is saying that the theological unity of proclamation of the Word and celebration of the consecrated bread and wine have moral implications. These interlocking moral implications have, as yet, not been fully clarified.

Although the bishops at Vatican II clearly stressed a deeper appreciation of the word of God, the Vatican II bishops, just as the Roman Catholic bishops who preceded them, had never addressed the central role of the word of God that the churches of the Reformation had stressed in such a profound way. This emphatic interaction between Eucharist and word is part of the newness engendered by Vatican II. Before Vatican II, many Catholic liturgical scholars had already done much by way of research and planning. This research and planning included a strong interplay between the table of the word and the table of the bread and wine. The Vatican II bishops inherited this material and made it their own.

The Roman Catholic emphasis on sacrament and the Protestant emphasis on the word of God have a long and antagonistic

---

5. Jean-Jacques von Allmen, *Preaching and Congregation* (London: SCM, 1962), 32.

history. During the time of the Reformation and the Council of Trent, small books on a "theology of the church" began to appear. This theological focus on *church*, which we today call *ecclesiology*, was something new. During the scholastic period of theology before the Reformation, theologians constructed lengthy treatises on God *(De Deo)*, on the Trinity *(De Trinitate)*, and on the sacraments *(De Sacramentis)*. None of the great scholastic theologians composed a small book on the Church *(De Ecclesia)*. In itself, this omission is somewhat surprising. Naturally, all of these medieval theologians mentioned the Church here and there throughout their writings, but none of them had ever gathered these aspects of Church life into a unified treatise such as those on God, Trinity, and sacraments.

When the Western Church suffered the divisive turn at the Reformation and several "alternative" churches began to appear, Catholic and Protestant theologians began to write treatises on the theology of Church. Both the Catholic and the Protestant treatises were apologetic in tone, for their respective authors wanted to defend their respective positions. Even more than merely defending their positions, these same authors wanted to denigrate the position of the "other" church. All of these theologies of the church were in some degree or another written *in patent opposition* to the theology of the *"other* church."

The Roman Catholic theologians defined their theology of Church as the only true Church and they did this by stressing the well-known four marks of the Church: one, holy, catholic, and apostolic. In their explanation of these four marks, most Catholic theologians singled out the "apostolic mark" as the most important mark of the true Church. These theologians argued as follows. The Roman Catholic Church was the only true church because the Catholic pope and bishops were the successors of the apostles. The leaders of the Catholic Church were the direct descendants of the founding apostles. The leaders of the Protestant Churches, the Catholic theologians stressed, were for the most part not even called *bishops,* and therefore their leaders could not trace their validity back to the apostles. The leadership of these Protestant Churches was *not apostolic*. This form of argument for the "apostolic trueness" of the Roman Catholic Church was echoed repeatedly in theological textbooks from the end of the sixteenth century until Vatican II. With the apostles on the side of the Catholic Church but not on the side of the Protestant churches, the Catholic Church had to be the one true Church.

In contrast to this ecclesiology, the churches of the Reformation stressed their own validity as true church by means of the word of God. All faith, all revelation, and all theology are based on God's word. The church itself has no meaning if the church is not based on and revelatory of the word of God. The word of God is the foundation and essence of any and every true Christian church. In their argumentation, the Protestant churches were based on the very word of God. The Vatican Church, so the Protestants maintained, was based on the words of the popes and the bishops. The Catholic claim to be the only one, holy, catholic, and apostolic church is based on a faulty understanding, since the main basis was the apostolic lineage of popes and bishops. But how did Catholic scholars prove such lineage? The Protestant answer was this: popes and bishops said so. Therefore, the basis of the Catholic Church is not on the word of God, but on the words of popes and bishops.

From the late sixteenth century onward, this battle over word of God/words of men continued, as did the battle of apostolic foundation and the lack thereof. There were practical consequences to this antagonism. In stressing apostolic and hierarchical succession, Catholic leaders emphasized one of the most important hierarchical ministries, namely, the celebration of the Eucharist. Since the definition of priest, developed by the scholastic theologians and institutionalized by the Council of Trent, maintained that only a priest could celebrate the Eucharist, the Mass—and this meant the eucharistic part of the Mass, not the "Mass of the catechumens"—became the major centering of Church life, of sacramental life, and of personal spirituality. The pope himself, as a priest, was of the same "order" as a newly ordained priest. As far as priesthood was concerned, this theology indicated that priesthood was the highest order of the sacrament and consequently as priests all were equal. Jurisdictionally, the pope and the bishops were institutionally higher than priests. This stress on Eucharist, priest, and priestly spirituality far outweighed any Catholic stress on the word of God. From the sixteenth century until the twentieth century, lay men and women were not encouraged to read the Bible on their own. To read Scripture, they needed the guidance of priests and bishops. In other words, there was a hierarchical surveillance on the interpretation of the written word of God. No offense to the word of God was intended by all this. The hierarchical surveillance was a precaution rather than a disregard for God's word.

However, in those four hundred and some years since the Council of Trent, the Catholic community was centered on sacraments, particularly the sacrament of the Eucharist, and even in a more particular way, on the "eucharistic part" of the Mass, not on the "word part" of the Mass. This eucharistic-centered community called Church did not exhibit what we call today a fully "gospel community." The emphasis on sacrament indicated that if Catholics attended Mass regularly and received holy Communion at least once a year, the Church community was exemplary. The Mass remained the domain of the clergy and the layperson was largely an onlooker. Eucharistic spirituality, during these same four hundred and some years, was focused almost exclusively on the priest. Lay spirituality was generally nourished by devotions.

The Protestant experience during this same period of time was quite different. For the Protestant churches, spirituality developed from hearing the word of God and living it. In the Anglican communities and in some Protestant communities, spirituality might be eucharistic-oriented, but in most Protestant communities the Eucharist was celebrated only a few times each year. On a week-to-week basis, it was the word of God that was emphasized. Many holy men and women—all Anglicans and Protestants—lived during those four hundred years. Their holiness was word-nourished, and their holiness was deeply genuine. Catholics today often are amazed at the spiritual depths of such Protestants, since these holy men and women were only infrequently nourished by the Eucharist. Protestants today are amazed that there have been many holy Catholic men and women who were not enriched on a daily basis by the very word of God. Interestingly enough, it is this depth of spirituality, Protestant and Catholic, that more than anything else has created an ecumenical reverence for one another. Theological agreements are honored, but it is the spirituality of both Protestant and Catholic that provided the more conclusive argument.

Although the bishops at Vatican II stressed the reading of the word of God for all sacramental celebrations, the reading of the word of God can be omitted in the sacraments of reconciliation and anointing of the sick, and the reading of the word of God is ancillary in the new rubrics for baptism and confirmation. Even for the Eucharist, the first part of the "integral" liturgy is not totally integrated with the eucharistic prayer, the second part of the liturgy. Somehow, the encouragement of the bishops at Vatican II on the role of God's word has been heard but not generously put into practice.

However, for Christian spirituality the word of God is central. Many saints reflected in solitude on the word of God. In doing this, they were often set apart from all other people, within the confines of their own living quarters or outside but in an eremitical place—that is, on a mountain, by a lake, and so on. In meditation, these saints were caught up in the unitive way. The peak of their spiritual journey took place, not at a eucharistic celebration but at a time when they were deeply meditating all alone on gospel life. Clearly, in the Roman Catholic tradition, respect for the word of God has never been lacking, but it has not, in day-to-day living, been central. Catholic hierarchical leadership, until the present postconciliar time, had not advocated a word spirituality. Currently, lay men and women are encouraged to read the Bible. Faith-sharing groups have been encouraged, and often at these faith-sharing meetings sections from the Bible have been read aloud and then those in attendance have exchanged their thoughts on the biblical text and its personal meaning with one another. Contemporary lay men and women have become, slowly but surely, more conversant with biblical texts and their interpretations. To some degree a word-centered spirituality has begun to develop. The union between a word-centered spirituality and a Eucharist-centered spirituality is still in its infancy.

Contacts with Protestants have been a major help on this issue of a word-centered spirituality. Many Protestants have shared their personal appreciation of God's word in their lives. We Catholics cannot help but be amazed at how easily the word of God has formed and reformed their spiritual depths. When Catholics experience a spiritual dryness, they most often turn to the sacraments for a renewal of their spiritual life. Catholic spirituality is sacrament-centered, while Protestant spirituality is word-of-God–centered. In the word of God, Jesus, the Word made flesh, is really present. In the eucharistic prayer at the celebration of Mass, Jesus, the same Word made flesh, is also really present. Our task is to make this Real Presence of Jesus "totally integrated," to use the Vatican II expression.

The Eucharist of the World
and the Eucharist of the Altar

The Eucharist is a meal, in which we celebrate the communion of people eating together. They are eating the fruit of the earth and the work of human hands. They are tasting the spiritual depths of the mystical body of Jesus. Too often, as people go out from the church, the Eucharist is over. Eucharist and Church are seen as one. World and Eucharist are not readily united. Theologians, such as Juan Luis Segundo (1925–1996) and Karl Rahner (1904–1984), have raised marvelous insights about the Eucharist of the world. Already in the thirteenth century, the Franciscan theologian, Saint Bonaventure, spoke about the three books that every Christian in his or her journey to God must read each day: the book of Creation, the book of the gospels, and the book of one's own personal experience. A full spirituality takes into account the book that the creator God spreads before us each day in the various worlds in which we we live. All things have been made by this loving God, and therefore we find brothers and sisters far beyond the Church, and we find sacraments far beyond the seven. If we miss seeing God in our fellow men and women, if we miss seeing God in the world about us, how can we say with any surety that we really do see God, but only in the confines of the Roman Catholic Church? God, the creator of all, is not limited to the Church. If we do not read and meditate on the gospels, the word of God, we will miss what God, the loving parent, is saying to us. God speaks beyond the sacraments, although God speaks there as well. In a place of major importance for all Christians, God speaks to us in the word of God, proclaimed to us by others, and meditated to us in moments of private prayer. The word of God is foundational for Christian spirituality and cannot be set aside through an overemphasis of the seven sacraments. Finally, in the world we experience, there are moments of unitive contemplation, given to us through God's loving grace. The Pastoral Constitution on the Church in the Modern World *(Gaudium et Spes)* makes special note of this. Our conscience, this document states, is one's "most secret core, and his sanctuary." There each person "is alone with God whose voice echoes in his depths" (16). In this profound depth of one's own being, where we are alone with the Holy Spirit, we are reading the book of our spiritual experience, the third book, which cannot be read alone but must be read together with the book of the world and the book of the gospels.

Eucharistic spirituality is an important focus, but in developing that focus we must continually go back to the three books: the created world, the gospels, and one's personal experience. Eucharist nourishes, and the life we lead is a life in this same created world that also gives us life and to which we also give life. It is led, for Christians, within a gospel framework, and we must let the gospel, the word of God, speak to us. This gospel is written in the sacred Scriptures, but by our life we preach the gospel. In the lives of others, we hear the gospel, and sometimes it is preached and heard through words. More often than not, we preach and hear the gospel in a wordless way. Eucharistic spirituality is a personal spirituality as well as a communal spirituality. God speaks to us alone in the depths of our heart and conscience. Our heart or our conscience, then, is a third book on spirituality, and just as the Eucharist is internalized into our bodies, so, too, is it internalized into our own hearts. There, in our personal depths, God becomes one with us—the unitive way—and we become one with God. Being one with God is the primary goal of all spirituality. Sacramental Eucharist is part of spirituality; but spirituality reaches deep into the Eucharist of the world and the Eucharist of our heart and conscience.

All of the above should speak volumes to lay women and lay men. The book of Creation is not a priestly book; the book of the gospels is not a priestly book; the book of one's experience is not a priestly book. We are first and foremost human beings, and these are all human books. We are also Christians, and from our Christian standpoint we can be nourished by these three books. We are sacramental and eucharistic, but we are also part of the book of Creation itself, living day by day as we listen to the word of God, and spending moments of aloneness in our heart. In and through all of this, God can be united to us and we to God: this unitive way is the goal of all spirituality.

Conclusions

Christian spirituality in all its forms can never find a solid base if it is not founded on Jesus himself. From Saint Paul's Letter to the Corinthians down to contemporary Anglican, Orthodox, Protestant, and Roman Catholic theologians, the best of the Christian writers on Christian spirituality have continually maintained a centering in God and Jesus. Errant spiritualities have indeed appeared during the past two thousand years, and the primary reason for their errant characteristics is their lack of a God-Jesus foundation. Too often, these errant spiritualities focus strongly on a single devotion, a single church teaching, or a single form of prayer or celebration. In this book, we have moved from the errant Corinthians to a sacramental worldview. Paul, in his day and age, urged the Corinthians to take seriously the call of Jesus to love one another. Only on this basis would their celebration of Eucharist and their eucharistic spirituality be solid. In our day, we too are called to the same goal: to love one another. In our globalized world, this loving has a universal focus. The Holy Spirit of God works in all of God's creation, and all of God's creation is a sacrament of God's own presence. There is a Eucharist of the world that complements the Eucharist of the word and the table of the Lord. The Eucharist, for centuries, has ended with the words, *"Ite, missa est!* Go in peace to love and serve the Lord!"* The Eucharist does not end when the gathered community has sung the last verse of the final hymn. Actually, the eucharistic community is charged to bring the Eucharist of the altar out to the Eucharist of the world.

Eucharistic spirituality cannot be merely an inward-looking spirituality. It is, of course, to some degree. We must look inward into our Christian community itself. We much look inward to our own gospel values. But we must also look outward to God's creation, and this creation moves far beyond the lunar Church. Jesus, as the Light of the World, sheds light on all creation, so that we can stand in amazement at the depth and breadth, the height and length of God's compassionate love.

This volume has focused on the gospel community, on the full celebration of the Eucharist, and on the growth from these two realities of a profound, world-encompassing spirituality. The eloquent words from *Gaudium et Spes* capture this worldwide vision:

> The joy and hope, the grief and anguish of the people of our time, especially of those who are poor or afflicted in any way, are the joy and hope, the grief and anguish of the followers of Christ as well. Nothing that is genuinely human fails to find an echo in their hearts. For theirs is a community of people united Christ and guided by the holy Spirit in their pilgrimage towards the Father's kingdom, bearers of a message of salvation for all of humanity. That is why they cherish a feeling of deep solidarity with the human race and its history (1).

To this eloquent call, Saint Paul would say "Amen!" To this eloquent call, we, too, the people of God, say "Amen!"

Works Cited

Audet, J.P. *La Didachè: instruction des apôtres*. Paris: J. Gabalda, 1958.

Babin, D. E. "Toward a Theology of Liturgical Preaching," *Anglican Theological Review* 52 (1970): 228–239.

Bauer, W. *Orthodoxy and Heresy in Earliest Christianity*, edited by Robert A. Kraft and Gerhard Krodel. Philadelphia: Fortress, 1971.

Bowe, Barbara E. *A Church in Crisis*. Minneapolis: Fortress, 1988.

Bradshaw, Paul. "Theology and Rite AD 200–400." In *The Study of Liturgy*, edited by Cheslyn Jones, Geoffrey Wainwright, Edward Yarnold, and Paul Bradshaw. London: Oxford University Press, 1992, 355–362.

Caird, G. B. *Saint Luke*. New York: Penguin, 1963.

Cavadini, John. "Fathers of the Church." In *The HarperCollins Encyclopedia of Catholicism*, edited by Richard P. McBrien. San Francisco: HarperSanFrancisco, 1995, 520.

Chinnici, Joseph and Angelyn Driess, eds. *Prayer and Practice in the American Catholic Community*. Maryknoll, NY: Orbis Books, 2000.

Courtain, A. H. "The Sacrifice of Praise." *Theology* 58 (August 1955): 285–291.

Daube, David. *He that Cometh*. London: Diocesan Council for Jewish-Christian Understanding, 1974. Also, *Wine in the Bible*. London: Diocesan Council for Jewish-Christian Understanding.

Dix, Gregory. *The Shape of the Liturgy*. New York: Seabury, 1982.

Fitzmyer, J. "Pauline Theology." In *The New Jerome Biblical Commentary*, edited by R. Brown, J. Fitzmyer, and R. Murphy. Englewood Cliffs, NJ: Prentice Hall, 1990), 1382–1416.

Works Cited

Flannery, Austin. *Vatican Council II: Volume 1: The Conciliar and Post Conciliar Documents*, Northport, NY: Costello Publishing, 1996.

Guinan, Michael. *The Franciscan Vision and the Gospel of John*. St. Bonaventure, NY: The Franciscan Institute, 2006.

Halliburton, R.J. "The Patristic Theology of the Eucharist." In *The Study of Liturgy*, edited by Cheslyn Jones, Geoffrey Wainwright, Edward Yarnold, and Paul Bradshaw. London: Oxford University Press, 1992, 245–251.

Harrington, Daniel D. "The Gospel According to Mark." In *The New Jerome Biblical Commentary*, edited by R. Brown, J. Fitzmyer, and R. Murphy. Englewood Cliffs, NJ: Prentice Hall, 1990, 596–629.

Hayes, Zachary. "Bonaventure: Mystery of the Triune God." In *The History of Franciscan Theology*, edited by Kenan Osborne. St. Bonaventure, NY: The Franciscan Institute, 1994, 39–125.

Howell, Clifford. "From Trent to Vatican II." In *The Study of Liturgy*, edited by Cheslyn Jones, Geoffrey Wainwright, Edward Yarnold, and Paul Bradshaw. London: Oxford University Press, 1992, 285–94.

Jeremias, Joachim. *Eucharistic Words of Jesus*. London, SCM, 1966.

_____. *The Eucharistic Words of Jesus*. Translated by Norman Perrin. Philadelphia: Fortress, 1966.

Jones, C.P.M. "The Eucharist: The New Testament," In *The Study of Liturgy*. Revised by C. J. A. Hickling. Edited by Cheslyn Jones, Geoffrey Wainwright, Edward Yarnold, and Paul Bradshaw. London: Oxford University Press, 1992, 184–209.

Karris, Robert. "The Gospel According to Luke." In *The New Jerome Biblical Commentary*, edited by R. Brown, J. Fitzmyer, and R. Murphy. Englewood Cliffs, NJ: Prentice Hall, 1988), 722–767.

Léon-Dufour, Xavier. *Sharing the Eucharistic Bread: The Witness of the New Testament*. Translated by Matthew O'Connell. New York: Paulist Press, 1987.

Maloney, Frances. "Johannine Theology," *The New Jerusalem Biblical Commentary*. London, England: Darton, Longman, & Todd, 148–149.

Marsili, Salvatore, et al. "Teologia della celebrazione dell'eucaristia." In *La Liturgia, Eucaristica: telogia e storia della celebrazione*. Genoa: Casa Editrice Marietti, 1983, 11–186.

McBrien, Richard P. *Catholicism*. San Francisco: HarperSanFrancisco, 1994, 480.

Mitchell, Nathan. *Cult and Controversy: The Worship of the Eucharist Outside Mass*. New York: Pueblo Publishing, 1982.

Murphy-O'Connor, Jerome. "The First Letter to the Corinthians." In *The New Jerome Biblical Commentary*, edited by R. Brown, J. Fitzmyer, and R. Murphy. Englewood Cliffs, NJ: Prentice Hall, 1990, 798–815.

———. *St. Paul's Corinth: Texts and Archaeology*. 3rd ed rev. Collegeville, MN: Liturgical Press, 2002.

———. "Eucharist and Community in First Corinthians." *In Living Bread, Saving Cup*, edited by R. Kevin Seaoltz. Collegeville, MN: Liturgical Press, 1982, 1–29.

Noakes, K.W. "From the Apostolic Fathers to Irenaeus." In *The Study of Liturgy*, edited by Cheslyn Jones, Geoffrey Wainwright, Edward Yarnold, and Paul Bradshaw. London: Oxford University Press, 1992, 210–213.

Norén, Carol M, "The Word of God in Worship: Preaching in Relationship to Liturgy," in *The Study of Liturgy*, edited by Cheslyn Jones, Geoffrey Wainwright, Edward Yarnold, and Paul Bradshaw. London: Oxford University Press, 1992, 31–51.

Osborne, Kenan. "Envisioning a Theology of Ordained and Lay Ministry," in *Ordering the Baptismal Priesthood*, ed. Susan Wood. Collegeville, MN: Liturgical Press, 2003, 195–227.

———. *Priesthood: A History of the Ordained Ministry in the Roman Catholic Church*. New York: Paulist Press, 1988; reprinted by Wipf & Stock, Eugene, OR, 2002.

———. *Sacramental Theology*. New York: Paulist Press, 1988.

Pelikan, Jaroslav. *Spirit Versus Structure: Luther and the Institutions of the Church*. New York: Harper and Row, 1968.

Perkins, Pheme. "The Gospel According to John." In *The New Jerome Biblical Commentary*, edited by R. Brown, J. Fitzmyer, and R. Murphy. Englewood Cliffs, NJ: Prentice Hall, 1990, 942–985.

Principe, Walter. "St. Thomas Aquinas." In *The HarperCollins Encyclopedia of Catholicism*, edited by Richard P. McBrien. San Francisco: HarperSanFrancisco, 1995, 83–89.

Radbertus, Paschasius. *De Corpore et Sanguine Domini*. Turnhout: Brepols, 1969.

Works Cited

Rahner, Karl. *Kirche und Sakrament.* Freiburg-in-Breisgau: Herder, 1963.

Schillebeeckx, Eduard. *Christ the Sacrament of the Encounter with God.* New York: Sheed and Ward, 1963.

_____. "Word and Sacrament and the Church," *Listening* (Winter 1969), 25–38.

Schmidt, K. L. "εκκλησία." in *The Theological Dictionary of the New Testament.* Vol. III, edited by Gerhard Kittel. Grand Rapids, MI: Wm. D. Eedrmans Publishing, 1965, 501–536.

Semmelroth, Otto. *Die Kirche als Ursakrament.* Frankfurt am Main: Josef Knecht, 1953.

Strynkowski, John. "Real Presence." In *The HarperCollins Encyclopedia of Catholicism*, edited by Richard P. McBrien. San Francisco: HarperSanFrancisco, 1995, 1080.

von Allmen, Jean-Nacques. *Preaching and Congregation.* London: SCM, 1962.

Index

Index

cause
efficient 70, 71
final 70, 71
formal 70
Cavadini, John 62, 127
celibacy 51
Central America 50, 51, 105
Chalcedon 47, 98
Chore-episkopos 41
Christ 7, 11, 13–15, 17–19, 58,
73, 91, 107, 115, 125, 129
blood of 68, 70, 71, 75, 79,
81, 90
body of 11, 68, 107
Christ-centered community 7
Christ-event 13
Christology 16, 47, 71, 79
Church
Catholic 4, 39, 40, 53, 55, 56,
66, 68, 81, 83–85, 87, 88,
117, 118, 122, 129
conciliar 16, 34, 75, 95, 99,
113–114. *See also* Vatican II
early 3, 4, 35–39, 41, 43–47,
49–53, 55, 57, 59–65, 69,
78, 85, 112
Eastern 87, 88
Fathers of 36, 40, 62, 81, 112,
127
history 36, 43, 55, 65, 67, 102,
106, 108
leaders 2, 36, 39, 40, 45, 50–
52, 55, 61, 99, 105
lunar 96, 98, 111, 125
monastic 80, 89
postconciliar 15, 98–100, 103,
111, 121. *See also* Vatican II
rural 41–42, 52, 105
true 44, 53, 55, 86, 117, 118
Western 65, 68–69, 83, 85,
87–88, 102, 110, 117
Clement of Alexandria 38, 40, 48

clergy 15, 43, 76–78, 82, 89, 90,
111, 119
collatio 43
conciliar. *See* Church
consecration 63, 70, 76, 78, 80–
82, 115, 116
Constance, Council of 98
Constantine 38, 62
Constantinople 47, 87, 98
Council of 47, 98
Constitution on the Sacred
Liturgy. See *Sacrosanctum
Concilium*
Corinthians
Book of 1, 6, 8–15, 18, 19,
102, 103, 124, 129
community of 6–10, 13, 14,
16, 18, 29, 38, 48, 49, 53, 103
covenant 11, 13, 22, 24, 25, 28,
50, 59, 60
creation 15, 73–75, 122–125
creator 18, 122
cup 11, 18, 22, 24, 26, 28, 32
Curia 85, 95, 111

Daube, David 23, 127
deacons 40, 52, 77, 88
devotions 77, 83, 88, 92, 108, 119
Didache 37, 38, 41
diocese 2, 3, 16, 17, 43, 44, 50,
95, 99, 105
disciples 21, 24–26, 28, 32, 50
divisions 8, 9, 12, 15, 16, 53, 54,
61, 99, 100, 103, 105
Dix, Gregory 23, 127
Dominicans 70, 71, 85, 86
Donatism 43, 44, 60, 61, 85
Duns Scotus, John 67, 69, 71, 73

early church. *See* Church
ecclesia (or the Greek, *ekklesia*)
48–50, 56–57, 117